WRITING ON RAVING

WRITING ON RAVING

ZOË BEERY,
GEOFFREY MAK &
MCKENZIE WARK, EDS.

O/R

OR Books

New York · London

Published by OR Books, New York and London

Visit our website at www.orbooks.com | All rights information:
rights@orbooks.com

First printing 2025

Library of Congress Cataloging-in-Publication Data: A catalog record for
this book is available from the Library of Congress.

British Library Cataloging in Publication Data: A catalog record for this
book is available from the British Library.

Typeset by Lapiz Digital. Printed by BookMobile, USA, and CPI, UK.

paperback ISBN 9781682196281 • ebook ISBN 9781682196298

The manufacturer's authorised representative in the EU for product
safety is Authorised Rep Compliance Ltd, 71 Lower Baggot Street,
Dublin D02 P593 Ireland (www.arccompliance.com)

Contents

Introduction 1

hannah baer / The Phone Thieves 5

Linn Tonstad / Ascetic Hedonism 11

Isabelia Herrera / When Din Becomes Discourse 17

Zora Jade Khiry / Unspooled, or the Emergence of Miss Priss 25

Slant Rhyme / Together Non-Linear 35

E. R. Pulgar / Club Paradiso 41

McKenzie Wark / Civilization and Its Discothèques 49

Journey Streams / Afters Afters 57

Zoey Greenwald / Cigarette Girl 65

Destiny Brundidge / We Can All Live in This House 73

Frankie Wiener / A Berlin Welcome 87

cranberry thunderfunk / Born-Again Freak 95

Alice Hines / Sloop, or How I Learned to
Shut Up and Start Dancing   99

Simon Wu / Four Folktales   103

Harry Burke / Music Heals: Lydo   111

Zoë Beery / Seedlings   119

Kumi James / A Politics for the End of the World   127

Geoffrey Mak / Mexican Nights   139

madison moore / Adult Entertainment   151

Ev Delafose / Dancing Lonely: Becoming Black,
Queer, and Trans   157

Afsana Mousavi / Entertainments of the Moment   167

Jesús Hilario-Reyes aka MORENXXX / When the sun
twilights at dawn   187

Brittany Newell / Ghosts on the Dancefloor   193

Anne Lesley Selcer / from CLUB SPACE   199

MX Oops / Ecstatic Aesthetics: Mind Training
on the Dancefloor   205

Gavilán Rayna Russom / Moments in Funk   215

Chris Zaldua / A San Francisco Ravedream   223

Shawn Dickerson / Safe Home   233

Contributors   245

Endnotes   249

Introduction

Zoë Beery, Geoffrey Mak, and McKenzie Wark

You meet a lot of interesting people at the rave. Waiting in line, cadging a smoke, sharing poppers, or at kiki in the green room. You get talking. People turn out to have all sorts of other lives. Not a few, it turns out, are writers. Or if not writers, they have some sliver of experience with the rave that would be worth writing about.

We feel like we share something when we rave, but what? It turns out, paradoxically, that we share a lot, but what we think we share can be very different. We even have different notions of what a rave is, what raving is. And that's OK. It's a continuum of wants, needs, feelings, to which we hold with different degrees and qualities of intensity, and won't let go.

Two of us—Zoë Beery and Geoffrey Mak—started a series of readings called *Writing on Raving*. It felt like there should be a space outside of the party to share some writing, to talk about it, where we wouldn't have to shout over the thump and womp, where maybe we wouldn't be so drug-fucked. A third—McKenzie Wark—was in the first lineup and joined the group from then on. We've been running *Writing on Raving* for just over three years. Most of the series have been in club spaces, before the night really begins. We want to bring writing closer to the party. We want for once to do readings that have good lighting, a real sound system, a fog machine, even.

A good dancefloor has a curated mix of people. Whoever works door has to be a good editor. Door, like an editor, has to know the difference between two meanings of *discriminating*. She has to have a taste for variety and quality, for dancers who will mix well and know how to handle themselves. She has to know how to do this without discrimination in another sense of the word—conscious or unconscious prejudices around race, gender, sexuality, ability, age. We, as editors, learn from those other editors, on the door, when they let us pass, or don't.

Writing on Raving is, we hope, like a good dancefloor. There's different kinds of style, knowledge, interests, experiences. We put the texts together as they might arrange themselves on the dancefloor, or in a mix: congenial proximities, energizing frictions, ambiguous flirtations. We've put together some who are writers first and ravers second, and some who are ravers first and writers second. A good book, like a good party, is one where everyone has something different to give.

New York rave culture is having a moment. The music, mostly, is techno, certain flavors of which became the soundtrack to a dancefloor culture that is queer in a different way to house music centered gay nightlife. If the party is a good one you'll find a lot of trans people there, and a lot of people you'll have a hard time classifying at all easily. We like it that way. We want to document and annotate and celebrate, but also critique, this world we are all making together. Here and elsewhere. *Writing on Raving* centers the New York scene, but isn't limited to it.

Raving is nothing new, and it's been different things at different times. We're resistant to nostalgia. We're interested in what it is now. Still: we honor our ancestors. Techno is Black music.[1] The art of dance as we know it is Black technology. This always has to be said so it doesn't get erased.

This is a book for all of those who need the rave. Who need to dance. Who need that beat in their lives, or to have been in their lives. This is a book for all those who have journeyed through the night, through sound, through movement, through chemistry, into other places, other times, other encounters. Not all of them welcome. There's risk and hurt out there, and we don't shy away from that in *Writing on Raving*.

Sometimes, at the afters, tired and drained and covered in schmutz, we look around at our raver friends, and wonder: How did we get here? What happened to us? What is this tentacular, thrashing, swelling thing that we all made together? That thing now slumped and aching and coming down into its fragmentary, singular lives. There's a lot of answers to such questions. We've gathered our favorite ones to share with you.

Brooklyn, February, 2025

The Phone Thieves

hannah baer

When I go out and dance, I usually have a crossbody bag the size of a large envelope. It's black and goes over my shoulder, down across my breasts, and around my left flank. This bag has everything I need. Cash, keys, sundry things to put in my body when I feel too sober or too tired, ID. It's also where I keep my phone. Usually.

In late January I flew back from a trip to the West Coast and went straight from the airport to the club. I got in late and was looking forward to a particular party. I didn't have my crossbody and so instead had my things in my coat pockets, a loose black trench that I bought in Boston when I was nineteen and have had since then, over a decade.

I was dancing with my partner, so happy to be back in New York, and we were holding each other very tightly, they pushing me up against a wall, my hand in the small of their back, our bones and fascia vibrating with sub, our eyelashes on each other's cheeks.

When I reached down into my pocket during a lull in the set, something was amiss. My phone was gone.

I had heard about this ring of phone thieves some months prior from a friend who works security at a large club east of Bushwick Avenue. He recounted that the phone thieves had hit the club where he worked a number of times. The night of a circuit party, he said, he was finally able to identify them. At the circuit party, the crowd was homogenous; the phone thieves couldn't blend in with the sea of topless, rippling men. The phone thieves were obviously not part of the party, they were doing something else.

New York is full of places where you are supposed to be doing one thing, and then usually there is someone, overtly, or covertly, doing something else. Someone is sleeping on the subway car. Someone is playing music on the sidewalk. One use of police and policing is to get people who are doing something in the wrong place to go into the proper place. Part of what it means to criminalize poverty is to say that wherever an unhoused person is, that is the wrong place for them to be.

I suspect ravers feel that some part of what they're doing is subversive. You are not doing what they told you to do, because you are staying up late. You are not doing what they told you to do because you do drugs. It is perhaps embarrassing to admit, but this is something that I have felt. I am subverting by dancing. One measure of how much you're subverting may be indicated by how much the police care if you are doing it.

In the days and weeks after my phone was stolen, I tried to spend some time without this device that enfranchises me, enables me to pull up a picture of my vax card, pay to go into a party, log into the computer system at the psychiatric hospital where I work. Losing the phone, I lost my key to certain parts of reality.

I would reach into my pocket to dissociate while I was on the subway, and it wouldn't be there. I would think of the phone thieves. I would go to take a picture of a friend and my phone wouldn't be there, I would think of the phone thieves. I would go to call a car, no phone, think of them.

In the movie *Casablanca*, the eponymous nightclub has a sort of resident pickpocket known to the club owners. The scenes where he steals the wallets of the various customers serve as a sort of comic relief for the more real troubles of the characters in the movie. As with my friend who runs security and saw the phone thieves but didn't call the cops, the staff of the club in *Casablanca* know who the pickpocket is, and they let him be, as part of the ecology of the nightclub.

I never asked my friend who IDed the phone thieves during the circuit party what they looked like. I know they were many and I knew they were not circuit gays, did not blend in with rippling topless men, but beyond this I have no clue.

I sometimes imagined them as mothers and grandmas with large breasts and bellies, swaying, serious about their task. An undeniable and unified matriarchy which would make the circuit gays look flimsy. I imagined them as elders of all genders, slow moving with wispy hair and canes, wise eyes. Unsuspecting they would slip through the crowd and into your pocket. I imagined them as small children who could move nimbly through the legs and feet of drugged dancers, picaresque. I pictured them laughing and throwing the phones into a large sack. Maybe they threw all the phones in one of New York's many rivers, or crushed them under a giant wheel.

Last Wednesday, exactly a week ago, the NYPD announced that under new mayor Eric Adams they have evicted three hundred encampments of unhoused people. Videos of these raids are not unlike videos of any kind of terror, some police officers doing their work dispassionately, others seemingly angry or animated by dislike towards the people they were evicting. Encampment residents' belongings scooped by tiny bulldozers, put into dumpsters.

Illegal partying subverts property relations, but legal partying at forty-plus dollars a ticket does not. Having your phone stolen subverts property relations, but not using your phone because you're doing a tech cleanse does not. If we agree that we do not like the way things are, we must ask over and over again, are we subverting them?

The phone thieves are probably not luddite activists. My thought about them working in a ring is that the ring is controlled by a man who takes the majority of the profits and salaries his employee thieves at the lowest rate he can while still getting them to work. In this way, he would be like a nightclub owner or a record company exec or any other capitalist. I romanticized the phone thieves because I couldn't see them, couldn't see how they worked.

I have wondered at different times how the phone thieves felt towards the partiers. In the world where the phone thieves are an activist collective of grandmas and grandpas doing a ritual intervention on colonized consciousness, I imagined that they hold the partiers in compassion, and wish them the best for the new lives without phones. I imagine my phone thief touching me through my coat as she found me, saying in her mind "may you be free from the Jeff Bezos-ification of your mind and body as instantiated by this infernal device, may you be at peace."

Sadly, if the phone thief ring is a financial operation headed by a shitty man, a little Jeff Bezos of nonviolent organized crime, I imagine the phone thieves recruit feelings of dismissiveness and contempt for the partyers in order to make their task easier, the way someone whose job is to clear encampments in public spaces may recruit feelings of contempt for unhoused people before they disrupt their living spaces and throw their belongings away. I hope my phone thief made commission. It's likely that her wage was comparable to that of the door person at the party, or the person behind the bar, or the bathroom attendant.

Last night, before bed, I re-read this writing. I then dreamt of going to a bar that I have dreamt about before, Mariposa, a dive where you can get special cocktails made out of fermented fruits. In my recurring dream about this fictional place, Mariposa is on the first floor of a building, and the upper floors are a nightclub run by mobsters. In the dreams I go up the stairs behind the bar Mariposa, trying to see past the door into the club, but an older white man with a gnarled face and giant fists silently shakes his head at me. The gangsters won't let you into their club. In my dream last night, while getting cocktails at the special dive bar on the first floor, my friend Anne told me she had figured out how to buy the entire place, and finally the queers and freaks would be allowed in the club above Mariposa.

I woke up this morning to the sound of my phone blaring an emergency alert, from the police, about a suspect in the subway shooting. I was pulled from the dream by this awful sound and reminded immediately about the direct connection between our phones and the cops. In my dream last night about Anne buying the nightclub above Mariposa from the gangsters, I don't remember having or using a phone at all.

Ascetic Hedonism

Linn Tonstad

My mother, who turned seventy on Christmas Day of the first year of the pandemic, recently said to me that she had one regret in life: that she had never danced. This the same person who threatened to withdraw me from my Seventh-day Adventist Christian high school when, at sixteen, I admitted that I had gone to my first club. We eventually compromised: I was allowed to stay in high school with my friends if I paid for two months of tuition myself, using money I had earned in my summer job.

Of course, at the time I couldn't dance, though in the club I had moved awkwardly to the beat of one of the top hits on the Norwegian charts at the time, a song called "støveldancen" (the boot dance), performed by a group of men dressed as nisser on a fake countdown-to-Christmas reality show on national television. Nisse can't easily be translated, but it is as if Santa Claus was only the most prominent example of a type of creature that lives in your barn and has to be placated on Christmas with oatmeal porridge if you don't want him playing tricks on you for the next year.

I went to my first raves in LA warehouses and remote desert locations during college, licking liquid acid off lollipops while enrolled in another Christian school that forbade dancing—among other things! I didn't start becoming a *raver* until about five years ago, and I had only really become a dancer about a year before the pandemic rendered the activity around which I'd rebuilt my life unavailable, irresponsible, even murderous in the eyes of many. I didn't even know that a dancer was something one could *become*— certainly not that I could become—but it turns out that if you do something for fifteen to twenty hours, two to four nights a week, for months on end, you get way better at it.

As I learned to dance, I learned to see as dancers do, which is to see how flesh moves together and apart, how flesh is oriented in space, how bodies move toward and away from each other, how a dancefloor is created and coalesces, how dancers communicate openness, invitation, consent, or disengagement. (I prefer, by the way, to say "flesh" rather than "bodies" because the body, when talked about, becomes an object or a possible possession. One *has* a body; one *is* flesh.)

Scholars of religion have written endlessly overhyped texts about the rave, usually focused on similarities between the rave and mystical practices found in various religions, always making embarrassing puns about ecstasy, and going on about neopagan Israeli ex-soldiers making psytrance. It is, of course, evolutionarily true that we became what we are by dancing under the night sky to repetitive beats, for music precedes language and dancing forms the social. But the rave is not mainly about harmony and unity, though fleshy togetherness can be found there like perhaps nowhere else. I've learned more about people on the dancefloor than I thought possible to know. But what I love about the rave is how it enables encounters with, maybe even an ethics of, otherness, opacity, and antagonism.

In other words, we rave alongside people with whom we have perhaps nothing in common beyond the rave itself, with people whose politics we despise, whose haircuts we dislike, who fucking film us when we dance, who push past us with their sugary drinks and surreptitiously watch us making out with each other (and sometimes more). The rave is an *agonistic* commons that does not soften the sharp edges of difference into diversity. Rendering the body mobile, and giving up, at least for a while, the fiction of a non-animal humanity, can power the fight for life, survival, and flourishing, for another day, and another night. But the rave is not only for life; dancing flesh knows it is grass, as the text says, grass that wilts, withers, and dies. The rave is what it feels like to be alive, and all that lives, dies.

It's Sunday morning around noon, a few years ago now. I've been dancing, with a few breaks for resting, stretching, and snacking, for hours. I'm dehydrated and a bit depleted, but also in equilibrium, a trance-like state of free movement. The floor has been moving pretty well for a while. Most of the drinkers have long gone (alcohol, cellphones and straight men who travel in groups are the enemies of dancing). The floor is no longer crowded, as it was during the peak right around 3 a.m. There are a few "newbies" or "tourists" left, about to be seduced into changing their lives, but most people are experienced, wearing nothing that impedes movement or traps sweat, or dressed in a way that, when the lights go down and the movement intensifies, enhances the visual appeal of the crowd, highlighting unexpected elements ranging from the flashy to the mystical across the floor.

The next DJ goes on, and within five minutes we have snapped into place, the dancefloor coalescing, and we are *moving*, faster and faster, closer together, building off each other. I find myself dancing in a loose circle with strangers. As the music shapes us, we acknowledge each others' presence: seldom with eye contact, more often by responding to each other's movement in some way, until suddenly we find ourselves moving perfectly in sync, now four people so close together we would ordinarily be touching, but there's no direct contact, only ongoing and mutual intensification, doing together what can't be done apart.

This person here moves with flowing skirts beneath his beard and bare torso; *this* person here brings their genderqueer body into the center of another impromptu circle, forcefully expressing the fleshy power their race and gender expression might wrongly be presumed to deny them; *this* person here moves as if a priest, opening flows of energy to the floor. After an hour or two, it becomes clear that the body needs to be attended to, and I step off the floor to get some water, bend my knees, and eat some vegan gummi bears.

To dance, and to dance well, means giving up self-consciousness *and* taking oneself off the sidelines, no longer hoping that the world will open up and make a place for one. (Indeed, dancers make space by taking up space.) Contributing to the dancefloor is a matter of bringing specificity to it, letting the body move with others' bodies in nonidentical yet interactive ways. There's visible difference, of course, between the uniformly front-facing lines of low-level Berlin parties and the creative interactivity of Brooklyn. The best dancefloors depend on difference, ranging from unapologetic inhabitation of the bodily unusual (height, speed, or the like) to decorative enhancement with colors, shapes, and striking clothing, to the mere contribution of steady, reliable bodily movement, no matter how small.

Such difference is neither transparency nor opacity; flesh evades objectified knowing. But to participate fully in the best dancefloors also requires an asceticism of hedonism, a discipline that is willing to wait, to keep going in tired, fasting, depleted states, a discipline that knows that one's own greatest pleasures come only with the participation of others who might want very different things from the interaction.

There is no point in idealizing the rave, because the rave is flesh, which means it brings antagonism, difference, bodily limitation, history, and (non)encounter together. But the dancefloor has given me what my mother's church promised but failed to deliver: the *love* of flesh. I *exist* only because my mother, who came from the metropolis of Baghdad in Iraq, and my father, who grew up in the small village of Tonstad in Norway, were committed enough to a Christianity that forbade dancing, alcohol, smoking, coffee, TV, meat, non-cishet-married sex and reading the newspaper between sundown Friday and sundown Saturday that they ended up at the same religious college in Beirut, Lebanon, where they met and kissed for the first time—after they got engaged, of course.

You see, it means something when my mother says she wishes she had danced.

When Din Becomes Discourse

Isabelia Herrera

On a muggy August evening on Randall's Island, I stood in a field of Honda Odysseys and CR-Vs, tricked out with towering rows of tweeters and subwoofers. Speakers were affixed to the roofs or lined the trunks of the vehicles like light artillery, painted in canary yellows, blood reds and indigo blues.

This is Dominican car audio culture, notorious in New York. It is often parodied on TikTok, capturing the tragicomedy of living in this city. "Me trying to fall asleep in NYC," a caption will typically read. Or "The Dominicans outside at three a.m." Pounding bass bludgeons an unsuspecting sleeper out of bed.

If you live in certain parts of New York, this is all too familiar. It is the sound of bachata, dembow and merengue típico infiltrating every city crevice on the weekends. The cops try to shut the music down against the peaches and lilacs of the 6 a.m. sunrise, and a game of cat and mouse commences. It is a secret world of pleasure and protest, made blaringly public.

My guides that night were Carlos Cruz, the head of Team Viruz, and his wife, Karina. They wore matching jerseys emblazoned with neon green text and biohazard signs, their nicknames inscribed on the back: "Virus" and "La Bambina." I first meet them on an anonymous industrial block in the Bronx, so close to a waste management site the stench of hot summer garbage slices through the air and pours into my face mask.

Carlos is a musicólogo; enthusiasts like him own cars with customized sound systems, and at meets and shows, they are like D.J.s and live engineers, selecting songs and mixing levels for maximum effect. Some prefer clean sound: high-quality audio that allows them to hear the texture of drum kicks and the metal scrapes of the güira in merengue típico. Others simply go for volume, the kind that suffocates their challengers and makes your eyeballs vibrate out of their sockets.

"If you don't feel like it's strangling you, then it's no good," Carlos said with a chuckle.

On the drive to Randall's Island from the Bronx, Carlos and Karina decoded musicólogo terminology for me. There are instaladores, those who install equipment and auxiliary batteries in cars, which are known as builds or projects. Instaladores often own their own body shops, which are also home to sound teams, the groups that gather at informal meet-ups in parking lots or participate in judged competitions across the country, chasing trophies and bragging rights. Karina explained that people curate USB drives packed with MP3s; others design and construct wooden speaker enclosures. The process can take up to five months.

As we entered Randall's Island, Karina issued a warning. "Get your ears ready," she laughed. The thump of a dembow riddim vibrated against the glass of the car window. As I rolled it down, a familiar playground chant—the coy, high-pitched moan of Dominican dembowsera Tokischa—leaked into the car.

It was the Sunday of the annual Dominican Day Parade, and flags fluttered across the crowd. A thin layer of mist evanesced into clouds of hookah smoke. Empty Brugal and Corona bottles lay discarded on the grass. There were plastic cups of rum and Sprite passed among friends and lovers, full conversations held in the exchange of a smile, a hand placed on the back, a booming "Coño!" shouted over the music.

As a diaspora kid, you inherit a genealogy of smallness. It's a forced lineage, one that demands you to shrink yourself—to swallow yourself in the service of whiteness. But that day Randall's Island was anything but silent.

In his book *Caribbean Discourse*, the Martinican poet and philosopher Edouard Glissant reflected on the defiance embedded in Caribbean speech and noise, a reality that evolved from the dispossession central to the experience of slavery. "Self-expression is not only forbidden, but impossible to envisage," he wrote. "All pleasure is silent: that is, thwarted, deformed, denied."[1]

At Randall's Island, it wasn't just loud—it was Caribbean levels of loud. A sense of intimacy hovered in the air. Here, you could feel the comfort and kinship that lives in noise, in the excess of sound, in the solace of overtalk. This was an inherited aural insurgency.

Josue Manzueta of Team La Movie is newer to the scene. Coming off his day job at a T-Mobile store in Long Island, he rolled up to a parking lot near Flushing Meadows Corona Park in Queens, arriving in an otherwise unassuming white 2020 Honda Accord Sport.

He set up his radio and a small chuchero, a cabinet with speakers, tweeters and sometimes a horn, and swiftly assembled it on top of the car, rearranging the vehicle and its contents like a Transformer. His sedan has a custom license plate that reads, in all caps, "Q DULCE," or "HOW SWEET."

Manzueta was introduced to car sound system culture by his father. "Back in the Dominican Republic, he had a huge minivan filled with 10 speakers and 18 bass," he explained. His parents eventually immigrated to the United States, where Manzueta was born. "He took me to an event exactly where we are right now, like six years ago. And I fell in love," Manzueta said.

Team La Movie is still growing, so its members mostly convene for casual weekend hangouts. "I don't compete that much," Manzueta said. "But if anybody comes and tries to put their music over mine, I'ma turn my shit up!" he cackled. "'Yo, your music is wack!'" he pantomimed, grinning from ear to ear. "I just love trash talking."

Musicólogos who have larger builds typically meet during the day at car shows, where they have permits and are safe from the police. But those with smaller projects congregate after hours, informally, when team members are off work.

Musicólogos and the police are almost always at odds. "Either the cops come right away or they're already here waiting for us," said Eddie Peña, a twenty-one-year-old part-time instalador who runs Team La Movie's Instagram, pointing to a police van in the distance, its lights already flashing.

Sometimes, the cops will pounce when the music starts and order teams to turn it off. If matters escalate, confiscation is common, and it is a musicólogo's worst nightmare, especially if you've invested thousands to customize your car. If the police can't easily remove the speakers, they'll take the whole vehicle, and issue a court summons that could lead to fines. Peña said that musicólogos may have to wait months to retrieve their vehicle from the pound — and if they don't have the car title, it will end up at a police auction.

"I feel like most of us get really misconstrued [as] being criminals," Manzueta said. "And we're not. Most of us have nine-to-five jobs. We have an honest living."

This is a culture born out of a love for sound, for community—a cradle of belonging in a country that is difficult to call yours. It is an echo of the din that saturates life in the Dominican Republic, the kind that occupies street corners, highway paradores and colmados.

"I just love listening to loud music," Josue reflected. "I love people-watching. And there's definitely a source of pride there. I love representing my country."

On the last weekend of August, I saw a different side of the culture: an official car show at the Wall Stadium Speedway in Wall Township, N.J. This wasn't the relaxed afternoon meet-up of Randall's Island, a weekend get-together organized just to pass the time. This was a desorden—a commotion, a disturbance, an uproar. The biggest projects and teams assembled for an hours-long display of bravado, harnessing a specific kind of throbbing, vibrating euphoria.

Vans painted in neon magentas and pastel pinks gathered in huge circles, the speakers on their roofs locked in embrace. Swarms of spectators congregated inside the rings. As far as the eye could see, there were gallon-sized bottles of orange and purple nutcracker juice, gold chains and baseball hats. Car windshields, T-shirts and caps announced team names, written in capital letters: "LA ABUSADORA." "TEAM BELLO." "LA SUPER RABIOSA."

And of course, there was the music. Bass pulsated through the air, expanding, and contracting like heart palpitations. Musicólogos blasted songs over their rivals across the circles, hoping to drown them out. I heard dembow, merengue, salsa, and bachata—even the ear-splitting sound of an occasional Tiesto or David Guetta remix. But of course, El Alfa, the charismatic dembow star who has spearheaded the genre for over a decade, reigned supreme.

Adversaries stood opposite each other on car roofs, looming high above the audience. Their fingers curled into the shape of mouths, dismissing attempts at trash talk. They threatened death, mimicking a slit throat. A man dipped a bulbous black dildo in a red Solo cup and jiggled it in the air, heckling his target with his tongue out. Another wrote a message on his cell phone in all-caps and paraded it around for his challengers: "NO SON DE NA,'" followed by an eggplant emoji. Basically, "YOU AIN'T SHIT."

That day, among hundreds of musicólogos in New Jersey, I thought about Glissant, the Martinican writer, once again. In just a few words, he'd captured how we lived sonic rebellion in our everyday speech, and in our everyday sounds. "For Caribbean man . . . noise is essential to speech," he wrote. "Din is discourse."

In New Jersey, I heard the moment when din became discourse. These customized sound systems don't just make noise. They hold the spiraling histories of Caribbean orality, defiance, and conviviality within them. They collect our stories of migration, of lament, of melancholia, of ecstasy. Our claims to be and belong.

That day in New Jersey wasn't simply a competition. It was a free-flowing idyll, one that refused smallness and silence.

I wrote this reported essay during my year-long fellowship as an Arts Critic Fellow at The New York Times. This is an adapted and edited version of the final multimedia piece.

Unspooled, or the Emergence of Miss Priss

Zora Jade Khiry

I gave up on being the most dolled-up doll at the rave long ago. The rave is not about that. It is about dancing. Dolls dancing. If my outfit constrains my movements, then it could all be worthless. Sometimes, I make mistakes. I made a mistake tonight by wearing oversized Phat Farm jean shorts with knee-high rubber Ganni boots. The look was fab but not quite rave appropriate. Too much skin coverage. No space for air flow. The boots or jorts could have been okay on their own but paired together made me feel heavy after the hours of dripping and stomping.

The mistake was made because I had planned on going out, but I did not plan on *carrying*. There is a difference. Going out means any number of things. I use it to refer to the club. I can wear almost anything to the club and get away with it. Carrying in this context has two meanings: (1) raving, usually involving hours of perspiration and uninhibited body movements, multiple drugs, and powerful sonic technicians, all within a suitable location, ideally a warehouse, abandoned building, or under a bridge and (2) the literal act of lifting, sustaining, or transporting; doing the most. The best carries involve extensive preparation, acquiring drugs, car money, energy supplements, snacks, tickets (or, for me, list), and the perfect outfit.

I have one main objective when carrying: to imagine my body in the future. Juliana Huxtable is booked to play at [REDACTED], the most perplexing venue in all of Brooklyn. I have never had a good night there. If I am going to [REDACTED], I expect to leave feeling unfulfilled and thirsty. But I can get on list there. And it's Juliana. So I put on my jean shorts, knee-high boots, and a beautiful Missoni top with long, dangling ties that I wrap sensually around my waist. I am dressed for the club. Not the carry.

The first person I see at the club is Video Girl. Wearing a backless bodysuit with a hood pulled over her head. There is something so deeply sexual and mysterious about a hood. She finds me at the bar. I buy her a tequila mate and tell her how incredible she looks. She compliments my hair then leads me to the green room, puts a neon yellow wristband around my wrist slowly, so my skin doesn't get stuck to the adhesive, and cuts me lines of coke and ketamine. She tells me that Mother (Juliana) is playing another set at a rave at [Warehouse] right after this one and she has a friend who is working door. But I am dressed for the club. Not the carry.

We finish our lines, letting them sink in a bit, the inside of my head expanding. On the dancefloor now, we snake through the crowd, up the stairs, and behind the booth. Juliana has just started. Her orange locs fall along her back as she whines her waist over the turntables. It's empty upstairs aside from us. I plant my feet shoulder width apart, sink my hips, and relax my waist. I can be comfortable here. For a moment. I brought the wrong bag. This Margiela clutch is not suited for the way I need to move (but it is fab). My body has plenty of space, but the awkward, annexed dancefloor with couches and floor length mirrors feels so impersonal, sterile.

The entire club does. We move downstairs to the main dancefloor and find a spot in the front. Same shit. Blurs of people travel rapidly in and out of the spot we carve out, like apparitions. Oh god . . . no. Some normies have pulled out their fucking Nintendo Switches on the dancefloor. Forgive them Lord, for they know not the gift they have been given, a chance to witness one of the best DJs alive spin at one of the worst clubs in the city.

I tense up, unable to dance among this bedlam. Not everyone goes out for freedom. Some people, perhaps even most people, go out for spectacle, to be it or to find it, and to hold those of us freedom-seekers hostage. Some people don't want to get free.

I head back behind the booth. Juliana is tearing now. It's a light tear. The cosmic tear will come later in the morning. For now, I am good. After another bump of kundle, I am surrounded by dolls on all sides. "What's your name, baby?" "Doll." "Me too." We go hard for Juliana, throwing our wrists into the air, shouting exclamations of ecstasy as the bass finally drops after a sexy break. I see Video Girl again, on the other side of the exclusive section. I dance over to her, taking in her movements as I make mine. Fuck . . . She looks so good. Maybe I will carry tonight. Just for her. We both have enough space to flow with the entirety of our bodies, involving our feet, knees, thighs, asses, hips, waist, tits and heads into a slither.

Still, there is something about the way this space is designed, the display of it all, that prohibits me from losing myself and finding my body. As good as I look and as well as I dance, I am not here to put on a show at this showy ass club. That isn't really true. In New York City nightlife, the dolls are always the show. Our hypersexualized bodies are the out-of-towner's drug of choice. We are surveilled like celebrities, like criminals, and put on display like antiquities. We are simultaneously the sexiest, strangest and scariest part of your night. Fuck!—I'm too in my head. I let the kundle jumpcut me.

Outside now, across the street. Myrtle/Broadway is post-apocalyptic at 3 a.m. We lean against a random tagged building, hunched over into branch-like shapes, waiting for the wind to take us to our next destination. Elsewhere in Brooklyn. Right near the water. Abandoned warehouse. Of course. Let the carry ensue. Fuck these baggy ass shorts. We arrive and greet the person at the door. Kiss kiss. Cheek, cheek. Honeyed words. We're in. Fab. Video Girl leads me to a corner littered with stained couches. Another line and my joints begin to expand. We slink through the crowd. There seems to be endless space in the hazy mist of nitrogen and salt. Are we outside? It feels like a jungle.

Juliana is ripping the slit; her broken, frenetic beats make the palms of my feet tingle. My first instinct is to run. Or jump. To do something to release the tension from my body. She introduces throbbing drums underneath a patterned, electronic layer, and my hips sink. I rub my hands over my tits and press myself against the beat.

I open my eyes and Video Girl is in front of me. She is ravishing. Her movements seem to connect with my own. We lock eyes. I float closer towards her, fully entranced. Her body opens for me. I place my hands on the sides of her hips, not too eagerly. I don't know what she does to me. I don't do this usually. I sense that she knows this as she pulls my waist into hers, conjoining us. Our bodies are moving together as one now. I lift my feet with hers. She swings her hips with mine. Juliana commands us to move up, up, up, up and down, down, down, down. We dare not disobey.

Something begins to shift. The atmosphere unfolds and reveals a divergent plane at [Warehouse]. Only Video Girl, myself, and Juliana take space. I look up at her, our bodies clinging to each other. Our mouths touch and I am disarmed. We transcend further into this lush new landscape; our bodies climbing the walls of sound like hedera vines. Is this how circuit gays feel? Their pornographic bodies of leather and muscle coalescing into a beefcake. My massive, Black, transsexual body morphing into a supergiant, the sonic mayhem sending me into supernova, the gravitational pull of my Black Hole drawing my sisters and sister-lovers into me.

There are more trannies around me now, Black and older. They graze my shoulder with familiar hands, bestow a blessing with a soft gaze. One woman embraces me, cradling the back of my neck. "So glad to see you, beautiful." Decades of transdata are transmitted from woman to woman, doll to doll, with just the locking of eyes. The beat shifts again, a hard electro moment. I close my eyes and breathe in.

My path realigns, and my life arrays inside my eyelids as a technicolored quilt. I see myself in front of me. Boy me. A child. A mollusk. He has never yearned for a future because he has never yearned to exist. Then, boy becomes girl. Her shell is shed and left to become sand. She descends into a sea of desire. Never have I felt so sure of my own future than in this moment.

Black trans women have such an intimate relationship with death. Loss may be inevitable, but loss is not the absence of life. We live in spite of loss. I have lived and will continue to live, just as these women exchanging power with me have lived and still live. For as long as we live, so does this music. Techno; a music of brokenness for a broken world. A music of tearing and ripping and shredding and scarring. I have held the fabric of my universe together by strings of will and hope and torment and dreams and regrets.

Tonight, I let go of it. Now, it is cut, forever torn, no need to be rebuilt or tightened or braided or sewn back together again. I am unraveled, completely. Untwisted, out. Knot free. A spool of thread, unspooled.

This kaleidoscopic trance culminates with a two hour dance break as my high shifts from the hallucinatory stage to the dancefloor diva stage. I move throughout the space fluidly, left, right, middle, and center. I find friends in the very front, of course, and join them there. I stand by the speaker and place my Margiela bag on top of it. Finally, I can rest my forearms on the top of my head and rock my hips in rhythm to the beat. I love this part of the rave, finding a position to actively rest in exhausted ecstasy. Juliana is blending sounds of rhythmic feedback. I worry at first the speakers are going out until the noise begins to increase in pitch, crescendoing into a final blare. The crowd screeches as the music screeches, our limbs flailing to the heavens in mass rapture. She ends her set in something I can only describe as a hard techno, electro brawl. MOTHER! I look for my friends again. I must congratulate them on surviving this war.

We have no words to describe what just happened nor any energy to verbalize. So, we look at each other, smile feebly, and wave our hands back and forth while shaking our heads in enervation. "Tore," I whisper, and the mist dissipates and the light refracts. Back on this earthlier plain, I take stock of myself. Somehow, I have managed to successfully carry in this completely inappropriate outfit. My jean shorts are a darker blue than I remember them. My brown Missoni top becomes one with my brown skin, my erect nipples bold through the thin material. My bangs are wet with sweat. I watch a droplet form around a coil of hair and fall onto my chest. I am desperate for water. I go to the makeshift bar and wait in line. They are out of water bottles. Insane. I guess there are worse ways to die than from dehydration after a life-altering Juliana Huxtable set.

Video Girl and her girlfriend come up behind me. They want to go upstairs to the House music room. The vibe upstairs is cute, but I have been completely consumed. We sit in a room with broken windows and white people in all-black locked deep in indiscriminate conversations. Video Girl spots an old white gay man who she knows has meow meow. I sit down next to her and try to relax, reflecting on the last few hours. This in-between flux of post-evisceration is always one that I dread. I feel too high to have a conversation but not high enough to continue dancing. I should go home but I feel the urge to wring this carry out like a wet towel.

This urge can be dangerous. Every carry has its limits. I remember my first Juliana Huxtable set at Basement. It shattered me mentally, spiritually and physically. I found a spot all to myself on the side of the booth between the speakers and the emergency exit stairs. I spun and twirled and stomped and proclaimed. I sang praise. I exalted and exhumed and exorcised. For weeks after my knees hurt from trampling the uneven concrete terrain. I was worried I might not recover. I went out some after injuring myself, unable to dance freely and thus unable to release. I did bumps of ketamine in the Nowadays bathroom to try and numb the pain a bit.

Instead, I received visions, visions of my body in the future. In the first one, I felt about forty years old. I had a shaved head covered in tattoos that wrapped around my neck and broad shoulders. My tits were out, bouncing and breathing. I watched as ravers danced to the point of expenditure. I was the CDJs, the mids and the lows, the filter, the blend. Commanding bodies and minds through subwoofers. In the second vision, I had no idea what I looked like but I was alone, seated in a dark room. I was unable to move and unable to hear, but I could feel rhythmic bass vibrating the floor beneath my feet. Desperation had wrapped its tendrils around me. How long had I been there? Will I ever leave? Is this raveless abyss my exile? How do I get back to my body?

But now, here at [Warehouse], upstairs in the House room, I sit in my large, Black, trans body, expended but loose. Free. My body is an ever-changing vessel. She is sturdy and persuasive but open to my experimentation. She is patient where I am anxious and assured where I am apprehensive. I am constantly in awe of her abilities. I have been nurturing her, cherishing her more. I allow her to lead while I follow. I sit further back, sinking into the couch, trying to see where she wants to take me next . . .

I look up. The white gay man. Looking down . . . at me. His face contorted with contempt. He leans down . . . his neck winding back and forth. I have no space. He is . . . so close to me. Cold, gray irises. Dead-eyed. Slowly, he curses. "And do *you* want any? Huh, *Miss Priss*?" He says priss how people say *nigger*.

It takes strength to maintain my connection to my body. Can't lash out. Can't strike him down, spit on him, eviscerate his fragile, faggot ego. Just that quickly I am reminded of the price of freedom. My big, Black, transsexual body, hosting a robust, mosaic self, is offensive to the white world, a world not made distinct by the mainstreaming of anal sex or any sexuality or gender or ideology. My Black transsexual autonomy, here seen in the simple act of sitting in thought, is radical? What, exactly, is prissy about me? Is it my style, my sunglasses, my posture, or my clear disinterest in fawning over him? I won't shuck. I won't jive. Don't know how. And I will not apologize for that ignorance.

I stare at him over the top of my sunglasses and wait for him to remove himself from my presence. If I am Miss Priss, then he is a peasant, a heathen, a stain upon my sight. He puts his drugs away and leaves. Alone, I get up and dance to House music while watching out the window as the tech nerds and stay-at-home moms of Greenpoint emerge from their domiciles. Just moments before this, the only people that existed to me were Black people, most of whom were transforming and transcending their sex and genders. My utopic, techno-ketamine-estrogen tesseract shatters. The carry is over.

I look around me and recognize no one. Not even myself. I do not mourn the destruction of my fantasy for long. I can't afford to. This hostile plane is home, despite how unwelcome I am within it. Whatever freedom I found is lost, but I am familiar with loss. The pursuit of freedom, however temporary, is always worth the violence of its theft. This journey will be littered with boundless, brutal munitions intended to obliterate my vision, expel my body from space, and kill me.

I kiss the friends I can find goodbye and call a car home. I roll down the window. The warm, early morning air against my salt-stained skin hurts like truth. I sit back and close my eyes, trying to re-imagine my future body.

Together Non-Linear

Slant Rhyme

"Berlin's Juliana Huxtable returns to Paragon's mezzanine . . . ,"
says a blurb on *Resident Advisor*.

This is probably the oofteenth time I've seen the doll "play." But
let's be honest, who's counting? Anyway, she was in New York City
from Berlin to play two parties and while I had to be up inappro-
priately early the next morning for housing court—I JUST HAD TO
BE THERE!—nothing will ever stand in my way of losing myself or
from receiving spiritualistic messages from her. *Resident Advisor*
is wrong: Juliana Huxtable is a New Yorker returning to New York.
Plus, I was invited by a friend who works the bar, which means I
had the opportunity to take in the moment within six feet of the
legendary purveyor in the infamous "mezzanine."

2015 was the year for identity and transgressive performance.
Everything felt like an institutional edging of Identity politics, its
performative diaphanous blanket wrapping every(one) victim in its
emergence. It was the first year I witnessed Juliana Huxtable in real
life. Art Basel Miami 2015. She was a baby tranny sitting silently

on a panel entitled "Transgender In the Mainstream," in conversation with Gordon Hall, Kimberly Drew, and David J. Getsy, moderated by William J. Simmons. She sat with her legs crossed, arms folded, and smiled with an impish glee the entire one hour and seven minutes of the redundant conversation because she, like every trans or gender-variant attendee, was profoundly confused when the moderator evoked a performative "moment of silence" for Transgender Day of Remembrance (which was nationally honored slash celebrated weeks before the winter panel???). Juliana barely spoke that evening. Her presence was admired enough that when she decided to speak, everyone in the room paid attention and listened closely.

Juliana's identity and performances are (will always be) an exception. Without an identity category, she builds sanctuaries for society's outliers and marvelous misfits. Her reputation and engendered positionality represents the pinnacle of a flutter pulse and grant access to the soigne multi-hyphenate trans denizen-class to pollinate the dancefloor and to destroy the archives. She reminds us that there is no future for the rave space or art (re)production without us, if we—if I—cannot locate myself in its history.

(Escape) Paragon

I arrived at Paragon early because Juliana has the keen ability to draw inexplicably large and interesting crowds. Usually, the kinds of crowds that possess some sort of liberal arts education and a nostalgic pervasiveness reminiscent of "old New York" (no shade). But these girls are the kinds of ravers that are slightly older and only show their passports as IDs. The kinds of ravers that are still talking about important events that happened in 2015 (lol).

Half of the line is drenched in Salomon hiking sneakers, some kind of moveable spandex fabric, like biker shorts or Yohji Yamamoto and the other half: descended upon us in the Deconstructed, post-apocalyptic utilitarianism or Gogo Graham. Oh, and tall boots! The line represents everyone's relationship to the para-socialite. One half of the line exhibits Juliana's iconic repertoire as a performance and visual artist in the New York academic/art world, and the other: a reputable trans nightlife DJ.

"Why are you here? Are you here often?" I asked a stranger while waiting in line to enter Paragon. "I am here for Juliana Huxtable? Do you know her? I was supposed to see her in LA but didn't make it," they said. "Oh interesting," I replied. I ran inside, looking for friends with faith, praying I didn't miss her set. I screamed at a friend working the bar, we took a shot or two and I headed toward the floor. It was packed. I slid into the front and immediately entered a cesspool of all of the community's hottest trannies. We all stood before the decks but beneath the mezzanine, oozing in sweat and commotion. The girls closed their eyes and danced lucidly to the beat. But I am not feeling it, so I decide to escape the floor and head to the "green room" for safety and, let's be honest, to take more speed!

I received the text "WYA? SHE'S ABOUT TO TEAR!!" Naturally, I decided to have a moment alone before the highly anticipated cross-pollination and a long night of endless meaningful hypersocial engagements. I rushed back out, but the vibe was still the same: immensely hot and claustrophobic. On an addictive substance but without its aphrodisiac powers. The collective buzz was missing, nothing illegal happening; I didn't feel like a co-conspirator.

In disbelief, I decided to move closer to the music. I went upstairs and stood right behind the booth, in hope and fear of a portal opening and taking us out of our turbulence.

Merge

When I finally received the discreet location for *Merge*, I was triggered. A friend sent the address of what was formerly known as Chaos Computer: an arts collective and DIY community performance space, now defunct, in a warehouse on the water at the edge of Williamsburg. Venues of this genre, without rules or security, don't exist as much anymore. I smoked an American Spirit on my walk over.

When we move past the door, it's all happening! It's dark enough that I don't have to perform an identity position. No one wants to be what, or be where, they are. The underground doesn't particularly equate to the counterculture or political left. Rave is a post-socialist activity. Raving is spectatorship is performance is resistance to presence. The line for the bathrooms is so long it intersects with the floor. The bar is distressed, and the community-staff are on the ground consoling someone who appeared dehydrated, as if they were overwhelmed by too many uncontrolled substances. I am so overcome by the collective excitement and organized chaos that I forget to take care of my own desires and needs. Then there is an outburst of joyful clapping and uproarious whistling that reminds me that I am a tweaker chasing the night for a reason.

Juliana had woken up and it shows! She changes the track every 45 seconds, making it impossible to become too attached to a rhythm. Gleefully staring into the crowd and occasionally mouthing "P E R I O D," as if casting a spell on us. Upfront, standing before the decks are all of my favorite ravens: Ley, Zora, Geoff, McKenzie, J, Adriel, Will, and the parasocial muscle gays with their tank tops tightly tucked behind their oversized JNCOs. They are moaning while flagging their Chinese fans, as if they are trying to distill the precipitation created from the evaporated heat of the building into fog.

The struggle between intelligent techno and hardcore is always a bitter contest, but Juliana Huxtable never fails to sedate the dance-floor into a twilight-zone malaise. She makes it hard to retain a critical self-conscious analysis. Suddenly, I am politically neutral. All of my problems disappear until it is time to do my final bump. I'm rolling in a corner near the exit when I see small beams of light peeking through the cracks of the abandoned building.

There are only a few hours left in the night-morning-day until the hard truth that I could potentially become unhoused would hit me. At that moment, I am not concerned about stable housing or the conditions of how to maintain it. The desire to live feels like a political decision. When I glance into the eyes of the strangers standing beside me I am conditioned with instability, with trespassing in the dormant space, with dealing with the cops, with looking out for each other. We are on the other side. We are together non-linear.

Club Paradiso

E.R. Pulgar

After crossing the gates
We arrive at the broken
Table in the back
Under the disco ball
Where the ketamine rats once blew
An inheritance up their noses
The seat of the cracked out
Couch where the poets did whip-its
And lay on rose petals
Is gone
The first shelter
Of this old paradise was paved
To make a refuge for new stars
With an underground following
A bottle of tequila
And without an atom
Of gaseous matter

At their core

In the center of the pit

Sweat drips on my chest and face

It's hot like the bad room underground

Not Basement but the darker place

Except there's no punishment here

I fan the person next to me in purple silk

Who reminds me of another brown boy

Who stared at me too much

But wouldn't make a move

Boys

We could be in hot heaven if we tried

But what would I see

With my glasses on

Covered in fat smoke

Throwing it back under dim red light

In a room where I once read poems aloud

In the perreo party VIP

My partner notes the more

One is in superficial settings

The more superficial one becomes

I think of every night I spent

Undulating under a fragmented mirror

Laughing with plastic sociopaths and dear friends

Comforting them

Crying with them

Doing their drugs

Offering them water

I'm not done with that part of my life

I think of the elders
In Ibiza and the Good Room
Not the club in Greenpoint
But the place where you go
If you aren't a dickhead
I think of the divine partiers
Who saw god in the reflected grid
In the long lines
In lines on metal trays
In finessing both
In the sweaty mechanical night
In the glossolalia oontz oontz beyond words
I have seen suns I can't remember
I have bummed every smoke
I have walked around the disco
Clueless and chic
As Jane Birkin
In *La Piscine*
Which you should watch
I'm not a pretentious fuck for saying so
In fact I barely watch movies at all
I can't sit still
I spend all my time dancing
And scrawling notes down
To quote legendary gogo dancer Anna Maria Ricco
"I don't want to lose one minute
Of this party
In the beach
In the discothèque"

This shit got so sceney
I ground my heels to dust
Dancing for years then
All of a sudden I looked around
And everyone was editing
A glossy culture magazine
With dubious funding
And no money for writers
Or they had a secret door code
They were unwilling to share
It was Purgatory
Not that new bar by my old apartment
But the in-between where you are purified or stuck
I am usually the one with the code
When I have it I give it to a doll who needs it
For years I was called haus Madonna
Never in the official way
Mother for a few meals or a cigarette
I was an icon
A Madonna and child
But not the Leo who got work done
And whose daughter meanders Bushwick
Dragging her nanny to the toilet
At Mood Ring to make sure she doesn't OD
I do another bump
After the light comes on
I flounder the new earth made of bass
And everyone I ever partied with is here

The girls who cared for me
When a shroom trip went bad at Elsewhere
The guy I sucked off in the bathroom at Alphaville
The Virgo who gave me drugs
Introduced me to Amanda Lepore
And disappeared from my radar
The girl from Texas against the wall at *Unter*
Who I have seen only once outside a rave
Monte wearing a crown and voguing down
Their long black hair sweeping the forest floor
Noah who graduated Bushwick
And made it to Berghain
The legendary Celine Dijon
Strutting in her green leather bikini
And Versace shades at Tresor
All of the best rooms I've ever been in
Mashed together in a cloudy open space
That smells like jasmine
In the smoking area
There are sacred hushed conversations
Head nodding and smoke
Tired saints of the rave
I see you
Eyes crusty with powder
Laying outside under the purple dawn
Still tweaking but gentler
Where is your shirt
Why are you only in hardware store chains

And star pasties
In this version of the good room
The open plain of it is hot
Not hot like the bad room underground
But hot like Miami as the sun in September
Wanes from scorcher to endless summer
It's not swampy
Everyone is in a look
There are no palaces
There are no masters
There are no covers
There's a table with instructions
On how to best ingest G
There's a soundproof cloud to hide
And eat cherries cherubically
As the set goes ambient
I make my way back to the DJ
I run into The Angel
They pull me into another cloud
And when they kiss me in the muted space
Music behind a locked door
Booming in that perfect way
Present but not overwhelming
Heaven is not the new bar
That was 444 Club
And then Las Vegas
Heaven is not the gay bar in London
Where Jeremy Atherton Lin
Saw mirrors and cock above the stalls

The angel flies away
I rejoin the floor alone
Heaven is this
Sweating and heaving
Undulating and panting and water
Air rapt with amyl nitrate
The language of the body
And not the language of the tongue
Heaven is this
A blistering sunrise set
Surrounded by no one
Who doesn't want
To dance

Civilization and Its Discothèques

McKenzie Wark

Brooklyn, New York, the present: I see him in the kitchen, looking on, nodding his head, encased in its baseball cap. I'm on the dancefloor, with maybe fifty others, the molly kicking. The vibe, already good, now has sheen lacquered on, chemically. We're dancing, smiling, letting the music have its way with us.

I'm dancing on the makeshift dancefloor of the living room, looking at him in the kitchen, hanging back. Maybe I'm projecting, or maybe it's just the molly, but I feel like he's holding himself back, like something encases his body, won't let him let it go. I'm feeling empathy for him, as I've felt that resistance, and overcome it.

Newcastle, Australia, the '60s: I'm not from a culture that does much intergenerational dancing. Nobody taught me the steps. I dance alone to my older siblings' records. I love Motown songs most for that. I put the 45s on the record player in the living room when nobody else is here.

Newcastle, the '70s: I still love to dance, but I'm a teen, and I'm frequently teased for it. Peer pressure is a bitch. The boys call me a girl, or a faggot, and the girls join them in laughing at me. I internalize that jeering as a kind of shame. There's something about letting go of one's body, something about letting it dance, that doesn't belong to straight, white, masculinity, at least of the kind from which I come, and from which the man in the kitchen came.

Newcastle, the late '70s: It's late teen times. There are choices to be made: punk or disco. I like both, want to dance to both, want there to be a synthesis of the different kinds of movement they afford. I go to the punk show and then on to the disco, after. This is almost impossible to dress for, given the different sartorial codes. I never quite fit in to either world.

The local punk band—there is only one—offers original songs and some covers that have the sort of feelings teenagers in an industrial town in this era feel. There will be joy but always edged with melancholy, and sometimes a little aggression. The misfit boys dance to that, and nobody stops them. I am one of them, or think I am, at the time.

The local disco is where the girls are. The upbeat feelings are not so relatable, but I love the upbeat tempos. The music has more rhythmic complexity. I'm learning from the music itself how to move with it. I'm terrible at the rituals of heterosexuality that surround disco, but I love to dance with the girls, and since I seem harmless to them, and no competition to the boys, they mostly let me be. There's a self-consciousness I can't shake, no matter how much I shake my booty. Something discordant, something off. Maybe those boys who taunt me are right: maybe I'm gay.

Sydney, the '80s: It's not until I move to Sydney, the "big smoke" as we call it, that I experience gay nightlife. This doesn't quite feel right either, but I go, and I dance. Hi-NRG music is in vogue, which I do not exactly love. I prefer the straight club scene for dancing, particularly when Rare Groove starts to take off. All those classic soul and funk records connect me back to my Motown phase as a kid.

I live not far from the Navy base, in Kings Cross. Sometimes American warships visit. (We're an outpost of American empire.) I come home one night and find two African American sailors on my stoop, blasting hip hop from a boombox. As this might attract the attention of the police, I invite them inside. We talk hip hop. No clubs play that in Sydney, so I take them to the Watermelon Club. They do not appreciate the name. They're nonplussed to find, inside, a bunch of white people dancing to the soul and funk records they grew up with, the music of their parents' generation. They think that's hilarious.

This is one of the times I glimpse a repeating pattern in the kind of white culture in which I was raised. Not having a strong tradition of intergenerational dancing, or its own organic practices of inventing and reinventing dance with the movement of the times, it just straight-up steals it from other cultures, and usually from Black culture.

Sydney, the '90s: Warehouse parties, gay, with house music— another borrowing from Black culture. My boyfriend and I go. Do ecstasy together, dance and fuck, surrounded by men, mostly white, who have no inhibitions about dancing and not many about fucking. I'm starting to think that its straight masculinity that has problems with dancing, as there's a letting go, a submission to the beat, that involved. You have to be willing to let the beat fuck you, and letting oneself get fucked is the one central thing straight masculinity refuses—at least in public.

Berlin, the '90s: Techno music is a revelation. I first hear it in little temporary clubs, in the gaps torn in this city when the wall came down. The speed and relentlessness of it reminds me of punk, but it has something else as well. A kind of alien abstraction, as if it isn't meant for any kind of human body, gay or straight.

I grew up on various kinds of syncopated rhythm, where the beats don't fall exactly on time. Whether its swing or rock or funk, or reggae, one gets used to there always being a wriggle in time. In contrast, the machine-like perfection of the techno beat, falling exactly into place, seems weirdly displacing. If you're used to syncopation, then it's the perfect beat that can move the body in a special way.

The machinic quality in techno, and my attraction to it, is an intimation about something in my body, in its relation to itself, that will take me a while to understand. I feel at home in its alien grace. It seems to me that there is dance music for straight people and dance music for gay people, but I don't quite feel at home in my body in either. I feel at home in techno, which makes aliens out of all of us.

Sydney again, still the '90s: I find the local techno scene. There it's sometimes called doof, as that's the sound of the bass: *doof, doof, doof, doof.* We pile into a car with vague directions, gleaned from handbills or wheat-pasted posters in search of bush doofs. These are reaching for another connection to blackness, a different one: a technopagan connection to Aboriginality, to echoes of corroboree. Well-meant wishful thinking. We're not communing with indigenous spirits out here; we're scaring the fuck out of the wildlife.

Sydney, late '90s: I find the emerging queer nightlife scene. Unlike gay clubs, it's mostly run by dykes. Its weeknights in second-tier bars or a one-off warehouse party, sometimes with a BDSM flavor. I feel an affinity for this dykey, queer world that I can't articulate, and that it can't read on this masculine body, this body I've never known how to operate, this body which only feels in tune with itself through the derangement of the senses, through sex, drugs, and dancing.

New York, a new century: Fast-forward through the next twenty years: falling in love with a New Yorker, emigrating there, becoming a professor at The New School, raising two kids in Queens, coming out as a trans woman, getting separated, moving to Brooklyn, and rediscovering a love of dancing—as a different kind of body. Those jeering boys from my adolescent were almost right. My enthusiasm for dancing wasn't because I was gay, but because I'm a girl.

Brooklyn again, now: We're back at the house party where I spot the man in the kitchen, nodding along, not joining the dance. I was never reluctant to join the dance. I just felt awkward, ashamed. Like it wasn't a thing a supposedly straight, white male body was supposed to do. He's from the same sort of cishet white culture as I am, where men are not supposed to dance. That's for the girls and gays. Turned out I was one of the girls all along.

He's not though, and not gay either. He has to find his own way into his body, into movement. Of course, straight men can dance. In most cultures they do all the time. There's a certain kind of whiteness where it's off-limits, suspect. Finding the dance means a certain move out of the encasement of that culture.

Flashback to Berlin, the '90s: There's straight white men dancing, in this sauna of basement, dancing hard. Letting their bodies be taken, by sound, in the dark, intermittently lit. This feels a little scary, at first. Some of them are hard men, by the look of them. By the way they carry their bodies, they make me wary. But not right now. They're all on ecstasy. They let something go. They let something in. I wonder what they'll remember of this the next day. If it will change them, or if it's just a ritual outside the encasement, locked away in this time and place.

Brooklyn, the present: At the rave, dancing to techno. That intuition, a long time ago, that the alien quality in techno left some space for other kinds of bodies—now I feel like I can be present in it and present in my alien body fully.

There's some sort of affinity between certain kind of techno and trans or gender variant bodies. Like it quiets the noise of our dysphoria. It can work for other sorts of people too. I'm on the dancefloor early at a regular club, as I want to dance to the opener. What I perceive to be three cis straight young women appear in front of me. They're giggling, having fun, trying to find their way into the beat. "What *the fuck* is this music?" one asks. They fall about laughing. It's not their usual sonic habitat, but they're game to try it, and I love that. I love to see anyone let themselves get free.

It ought not need saying but it always does: techno, like house, like funk, like disco, like soul—is Black music. Started in Detroit, by Black producers, straight men, mostly. Their break came when they took their records to Chicago, where they moved the crowds in Black gay nightclubs. Then their sounds took off in Berlin and the North of England. All places where the industrial era ground to a halt, and with it the sensibility of uplift and upward mobility you can still hear in disco and house. If there was to be a future for anyone it would sound like something else, as yet unheard. That's what techno sounded like, back in the '90s: a Black future.

Over its thirty year arc, techno mutated and proliferated into a plethora of subgenres. There's business techno, the sound of financialization, the sound of digital money. I don't much care for it. What I'm looking for are sounds that aren't about a future return on investment. I want to dance to sounds that, through their relentless insistence on repetition over variation, invite the dancer into a sideways time, a pocket in time where there's more time. A place to put your body where you can actually live with the barely conscious thought that there's not many possible futures left at all.

The fragility of future time, the art of having to snatch your roses now while you live, that's always been something certain kinds of people have known all about. Where blackness, queerness, and transness overlap as marks of the excluded body, the taunted body, the endangered body—that's where you find the art of dancing one's way into the present to get free. When I came out as transsexual I took one step closer to that sensibility, but only one step.

I'm outside the rave, hanging with the door person (who's Black) and the bouncer (he's white). Door has been down the waiting line, throwing people out of it he doesn't think belong. Another rave friend calls this "reparative discrimination." This rave is for those not welcome elsewhere. Door comes over to bouncer and me.

Door:	"Shoulda seen his khaki-wearing white ass complain when I told him this wasn't for him!"
Bouncer:	"Hey, I'm white, and wearing khakis!"
Door:	"Girl, you're Caucasian. Being white is a *choice*. You don't have to make it."
Me:	"So is wearing khakis."

I hear my friend working Door on this. I hear the generosity on offer. Owning up to what whiteness did and does, not trying to hide from it, but resisting it at the same time. I'm still white, and have the resources from my middle class life—a steady job, some savings. When I transitioned, a lot of my cishet friends fell away. I found myself in trans community, and closer to, but not of, Black queer and trans life. Queer and trans life in America is as segregated as everything else. Our worlds are just so small they end up adjacent.

As my New School colleague Dominic Pettman puts it: "civilization and its discothèques."[1] Whiteness wants both proximity to, and distance from, what it takes from blackness. At the same time, whiteness wants to project onto blackness qualities it disavows as impediments to power and control.

Newcastle, the sixties: Nobody is around. I put a 45 on the turntable. Drop the arm on it. Smokey Robinson sings, but it's the bass and drums that move me. The way the bass bubbles around the edges of the beat, offering suggestions for where the body can move next. It's all over in three minutes. Put on another record. The Temptations, or The Supremes. I'm not putting them back in their sleeves, and I expect I'll get in trouble for that later.

Brooklyn, now: Surrounded by dancers, movements meshed. I found my way to the place where dancers offer themselves up to the dance without hesitation. It's five in the morning. We've been at this a while. Dancing to techno. The rhythms are not like Motown. It's a different time. It moves me in different ways. Sometimes it seems like every time you dance and get free connects to every other time, a sideways time, alongside, but outside all that history and biography encase.

Afters Afters
Journey Streams

I approached the dim facade of 59 Montrose Avenue on a bleary, nondescript night. I had heard murmurs of The Spectrum in smoking sections, in smutty pre-pandemic recollections. I glanced down at my *lewk* and began to second-guess myself. I texted my friend a photo. It was only 2 a.m. after all; I could go home and change. My phone vibrated: *You could show up in plastic wrap and glitter with a lawn flamingo on your head—it would be kosher.*

I stepped through the door to a narrow hallway. It was oddly quiet, but a distinct smell wafted through the heavy air, beckoning me down the hallway toward the world waiting on the other side. I was comforted by the words spray-painted in purple on the wall above the stairs. *Thank you for helping us maintain a safe queer community space.* It centered me as I ambled across the damp carpet toward the door.

As I passed through the threshold of the space, I was immediately disoriented. I felt the tile floor almost slip out from under me with my first steps past the bathrooms. As I caught my balance, a towering creature emerged from what could only be described as a urinal room. "Guess no one fixed the toilet since last week." She joined the fray, a perpetual mosh-pit of color and texture. There was a sense of renewed recognition in the eyes of the strange faces around me, seemingly reuniting again here.

The crowd expanded beyond the edges of the space, mirroring onto itself infinitely through the panes that lined the walls. In the deep haze it was hard to make out where the space ended and its reflection began. I slid between bodies, determined to make it to the bar just to have something to hold on to.

Five dollars down, and warm beer in hand (broken refrigerator), I turned to face the crowd again. The BPM increased, and I noticed The DJ, on the other side of the room, tucked behind an empty stage. He was chatting with someone with one ear on his headphones and the other cupped to their mouth. Our eyes met briefly through the mangled chain-linked fence surrounding the booth. His friend must have said something funny. He smiled.

I entered the milieu myself and moved to the beat. The hardwood floors bounced to a sound I couldn't quite put my finger on. It wasn't house, but the techno elements felt more rhythmic, more grounded. I looked up, and caught my reflection in the glare of the skylight at the center of the room. Everywhere I looked, I found myself reflected back to me. I scanned the scene: someone was really feeling the music, seismically shifting the surrounding dancers into an audience of fans. A crowd formed around the stripper pole. Someone was attempting to climb it, again. They slid to the floor, and the crowd went wild. It seemed as though everyone chose a moment in the night to put on a show.

My body warmed to the beer, and I began to meld with the crowd. The instant I closed my eyes in a small moment of bliss, I felt a hand on my shoulder. I turned around, and was greeted by a coiffed afro, a pair of sunglasses, and a toothy smile. The Photographer wasn't wearing a shirt, and his shorts were barely hanging on to his hips. His camera strap was tightly wrapped around his wrist. It seemed his lens never left his hand. He gestured to his camera, and I welcomed his request graciously, nervously. I blinked, and The Photographer knelt to the floor, and began flashing his camera up the length of my body. "You look fab tonight, dear." We kissed each other's cheeks. I admitted to The Photographer that it was my first time at The Spectrum. He looked at me with sympathetic eyes, then a confused brow. The Photographer flitted to review his camera roll, suddenly unsure of how he got here, or where *here* was. I blurted out a question: "Have you always been taking photos here?"

"I don't think so. No, I can't—no. I mean, if I were then there would be pictures in here. I was pretty good at keeping things together. I would hear this narrative of 'New York City's dead and blah, blah, blah,' you know, there's something to the idea that it is cost-prohibitive to be weird here. If you're weird. Then you spend forty to sixty hours a week working some job, and then you're too tired to make the thing you're working on. Whereas in Berlin, I've seen so many ambitious people go, and then it's a little too easy there. So the people making things aren't pushing as much in certain ways. You know, Mexico City has a balance, where you can live like a human, and then you can also focus on these projects. Sorry, the point is that there's always been this underlying narrative that the city is too expensive, not conductive to artists. 'New York is dead.' I've always named Gage as one of the handful of things happening in New York City that were finger on the pulse, pushing us forward. They're always creating safe, inclusive space. Very inclusive. People always show up."

I scanned the room and noticed a doorway I hadn't seen earlier. I excused myself from The Photographer and wriggled through the crowd as people around me found the beat in their bodies all over again. I exhaled into the cubby nestled to the left of the bar. The music was quieter here. The unrelenting sound now competed with the buzz of conversations that draped the air. Silver lamé haphazardly covered a couch and ottoman that furnished the room. I caught the eyes of a man in a shearling jacket leaning against the countertop opposite the couch. I had completely lost my sense of time, but it was clear he had been here for hours. His glasses were propped on his forehead, fogged from the heat of the room.

He flashed me an anxious smile. I wasn't sure if that beckoned an invitation to say hi, but I maneuvered toward the curious wallflower anyway. "Aren't you hot in that?" I brushed his coat in admiration and concern. "Yes, very hot. But I lost this coat here once and I'm determined not to lose it a second time. I found it upstairs where I must have left it, but that had to have been years ago . . . "

The Writer looked down at the jacket, then around the room, realizing he hadn't done the math himself. "You know," he started, "this place has lived several lives. To some extent it's true: The Spectrum exists within us now." "That seems to be the vibe tonight," I joked. "I didn't know what to expect. I'm just happy to be here."

"Me too. Or whatever versions of myself this place remembers." He sipped his seltzer. "However this place formed, how it came together, and what it was, will never come back in that specific way ever again." I absorbed his words, fixating on the grain of the counter. The tabletop began to pixelate, almost like a jpeg collecting dust on a Facebook page. The Writer began again. "I think what makes New York exciting is that hopefully new people always take the mantle and create something that reflects the next moment."

"It wasn't any easier than it is today. There wasn't better access to abandoned spaces or more free time. Its existence made no sense. It grew organically out of Gage's philosophical ideas about what it meant to be queer and how the queer community must truly facilitate diversity. That ethos was embedded in all of their activities."

Figments of friends from future lives bumped shoulders around us.

"I hope the next generation will think of The Spectrum the same way my peers and I thought about Paradise Garage. It was long before our time, but still the stories and music always inspired us. The Spectrum was special because it was created by queer people working outside of capitalism, collectively building a space for themselves and their peers where we could all share and propagate our creativity. It was done on our own terms. They showed that it can happen against all odds."

The Writer joined me to hunt for another room-temperature beer. A wave of heat wafted over us as we re-entered the dancefloor. I could only imagine how hot The Writer must have been in his shearling coat. As we navigated around to the bar. The music had shifted. Hip Hop blasted through the speakers to the elation of many around me. The DJ I saw earlier now trudged through the crowd, clearly intent on getting to the bar after finishing his set. He looked relieved yet weary, fielding praise and absorbing the love from the phantoms he encountered on his trek across the room. His face brightened at the sight of The Writer, and the two embraced, knocking the hat off The DJ's head.

"I was just talking to this kid, didn't realize your set was ending so soon." The DJ's eyebrows rose. "I've been playing for the past two hours; it was about time." The dryness of The DJ's tone was accentuated by the force of his British accent. He took stock of me, standing awkwardly as these two friends reunited.

I turned to order a beer and caught my hazy reflection in the mirror. I felt a drop of something hit my forehead as the mirror dripped with the sweat of the room, fogged by the humidity of the dancery. It almost seemed as if the mirror was dripping off the wall. As I turned from the room's blurry reflection, the faces around us began to melt to a familiar ambiguity. The walls were slick with the residue of bodies. The porous skin of its occupiers sublimated to steam as the room's haze grew heavier.

I noticed liquid pooling at my feet, at first thinking the bar's broken fridge was responsible, but I soon realized the entire dancefloor was flooding. Everyone danced on, splashing in the thick wetness, becoming a part of it. The pleather couch in the corner had disappeared into a bright pink streak in the primordial ooze. The music stuttered and skipped; the stage dissolved in the swirl. The DJ was nonplussed, prepared to say goodbye to the space once again as we trudged through the knee-deep slime.

"I knew it would be The Loft of its day, but we don't own those days. You can't be too precious about culture. People try to hold on to it, and especially here, people have gotten really obsessed with the origin of culture. Culture is meant to be absorbed, blown apart, reimagined. I remember, the crowd was only so incredible because it was like a secret. I've never been into the word, I've always been into the secret.

So as soon as the word is out, I'm not interested.

For a long time, The Spectrum was a secret.

And then it became the word

—and now it's gone."

Our feet lost contact with the dancefloor. We floated in the mix. The ooze brimmed to the ceiling as The DJ and I shared a last breath. I lost him in the translucency of the substrate. I could only make out the silhouette of the skylight, brightening with the first light of day. The music pumped through the thickness, vibrating gelatinous sludge that grew more viscous with each moment. The daylight split to colors as the mixture solidified, casting our bodies in amber. Sweat crystalized in deposits in this dark and shimmering mass left in the coagulation of cognitive phlegm.

Memory. Mineral.

What is left cannot be fully grasped, yet remains tangible in theory. An enigmatic shape that repels clarity and invites inquiry. It exists not as a resource for extraction, but a record of where we have come from and where we have been. In its refractive surface, the image of our present reality is warped and multiplied through this impossible prism. It begs us to count the number of colors at our disposal a second time, recognizing in its spectrum something that points to an alternative way of seeing and being seen.

Cigarette Girl
Zoey Greenwald

Kathy Acker, *New York City in 1979*: All the poor people who're making this club fashionable so the rich want to hang out here, even though the poor never make a buck off the rich pleasure, are sitting on cars, watching rich people walk into the club.

Anyway. Tonight at the club I'm carrying ice buckets up the stairs in my Disaffected Club Girl—the girl on the job, on hour seven of the job, wearing her eyeliner like an ancient wiseman trying to block out the sun or like an Aubrey Plaza character—as opposed to my Woohoo Club Girl, the girl who would've been at a lame party in Manhattan right now candy flipping or pretending to be candy flipping while considering the ethics of simultaneously flirting with the Gucci model I've got a crush on and the older artist who invited me to a sex party. No, walking down the stairs in my tiny-tiny skirt, two people look up at me as if I have interrupted. I walk past them, go dump the ice.

Later, I watch them make out on the security cameras. In the grainy black-and-white they look the opposite of whatever I suppose they feel: alone, away, mythic. In the dark with the smell of cardboard, I'm sucking on a lime, trying not to get scurvy, like the time Grimes only ate spaghetti for a year. In the hazy corner of the screen his hand is just barely visible on her leg and her thigh is sticking to dried vodka on the bench, pulling slowly. Like watching *Tom and Jerry* without the sound on. When he goes for her neck, he doesn't push her hair out of the way. She flips it, shaking her head. A little like she's miming "no."

I see worse in daylight. Like in daylight, when Ana and I were supposed to go see *Variety* by Bette Gordon, but she texted me: CASTING RUNNING LONG. MEET ME HERE? Skipping up the stairs of a building in SoHo, I arrived at a large, heavy studio. Even though it was summer, nobody seemed to be sweating. I was the only one in the room sweating, maybe because I was wearing a leather bodysuit. For a Marc Jacobs casting, I also seemed to be the only one wearing a type of *clothing* other than black tank tops. Feeling the sweat in-between my earlobes and my headphones, I was handed a piece of paper and told to write my name, height, and shoe size. There was no waiting room, and I didn't protest.

The shoes we were made to walk in: these seven-inch platform boots stopping two inches below the knee, rows of small buckles fastening the objects to our bodies. Looking at Ana, we were in some strange erotic game involving prosthetics, exhibition, and humiliation. I felt dizzier than I do when I'm drunk. Ana hates this kind of thing; the whole game; this production of images that is ostensibly a job, and before the summer is out she will email her agent that she wants to quit. But I wanted to be comatose in those shoes, like Winona Ryder in the back of *Vogue*. Winona Ryder is *short*, too. I was the shortest person in the room, the shoes making everybody already tall, taller—towering statuesque icons. The word of the moment: icon.

That summer I had so briefly visited Sky at school. In something that wasn't quite a dorm room but definitely also wasn't a real place, I said *I don't even want to be an icon* to the nonbinary nineteen-year-old who had called my outfit *iconic*. I sighed: *It seems like so much work.* I was drunk, wearing an admittedly great outfit, and being annoying on a college campus. The nonbinary nineteen-year-old was playing a synthesizer and seemed practiced; more practiced and sober than the haute intelligentsia who roll through the club with their bright blue Hennessy cocktails and Comme des Garçons. At the very least more dedicated and practiced than me, who rolls my eyes and falls carelessly into the designer clothing that my friends have laying around, too cool for makeup until someone's on me with it and I'm too busy loving whoever's on me with it to complain. There was still glitter on my eyelids from the club when I took the redeye to visit Sky. I wanted to imagine what it would be like to be a nonbinary nineteen-year-old at a real actual college, with a cafeteria and a library and a rolling green where things were comfortable and had comfortable precedents. Tragically, this was my relief from the world. I mean, New York.

Leaning behind the bar, I have a text from Flynn. NEED YOU. I've been running lights when Flynn needs to take bathroom breaks, cracking open a Modelo and trying not to spill it on the lightboard, playing the lightboard like a synthesizer even though I have no idea what any of the buttons do. This is a lot like my life. Oh, blackout. Oh, pinks. Oh, blues. Oh, strobe. I flick a switch and a tall, bright column of orange and red bulbs illuminates. It seems like it was supposed to be saved for a special occasion. Wait, I know this one. It's an exact replica of the light columns at Studio 54.

I never said I wasn't interested in history, even if I am too busy sweeping cigarette butts and pocketing half-full dime bags and ripping tights into bra-tops to participate in it. Sometimes, bussing cups around the club, carrying my tray against my tequila-sticky midriff, I imagine myself a cigarette girl at Studio 54—if cigarette girls were even still a thing by then. One time a man attempts to take my tray from me but actually is holding my ass under my skirt. ESCAPE FROM PLANET CREEPO!! But after he's thrown out by security there is still, somewhere, glass breaking. Isaiah asks me *are you okay?* I say *yes* unconvincingly. But then the DJ plays a track which uses just the rap part of "Vogue" as a sample. *Ladies with an attitude. Fellas that were in the mood.*

We do tequila shots. This is the best nightclub in New York City. Diving over the coat check counter I have a plan to consume, as quickly as possible, the entire bag of plantain chips I stashed there hours ago. I'm very impressed by this plan. But the girl is new and has lost all of the number tags. A dense, confused line of people begins to form and there's a moment I can see in slow-motion, but I can't describe that moment to you because it's already over and I'm being swallowed by mink and cheetah-print synthetic blend, North Face and anonymous puffer, giant glittering shawls, and black trenches. *Swallowed.* Have you ever seen a video of a snake eating an egg?

Surely I am part of the grand, momentous machine which is this club, pulsating through every late-night in time to itself. Pulsing, really: the beat, my trips up and down the stairs, the carousel of people in the shortening and lengthening line outside on the camera, all the metal cups. I refill the waters, and somebody says *thank you thank you hydration.* Like it was my idea.

Surely this place is a machine. But what does it do? Machines are for making. The ice machine makes ice. The synthesizer makes soundwave-forms. The club makes: culture? The club makes: money? The club makes: party? Is party where culture makes money? Is culture where money makes party? The club makes: culture. Like literature, then. Then, how am I read as a glyph inside the text of this club? Like literature, where *who're* can also be *whore*. Like everybody knows it: pigtails bring in more tips.

On the phone while I'm hacking away at a pineapple my dad's gay friend says, *at Studio 54 we used to bartend shirtless.* Me too, only I'm a girl so I'm wearing a pink bikini top. And everybody loves a good-time-girl, a Girl Bartender who wears next to nothing. Beyoncé Beyoncé Beyoncé. Everybody likes it at the club. Everybody likes a good-time-girl-bartender in latex. Zoey's not fast enough at juicing the limes. That's not why Zoey got hired here. Zoey got hired here because Beyoncé Beyoncé Beyoncé. Zoey got hired here because culture, where culture is fractions and culture over party makes money. I play fractions. I play good-time. I play in the goo of straining pineapple pulp-gunk with my black latex–gloved hand.

What are you doing playing in it like that.
This is why it takes her so fucking long to juice.

Maybe I've misunderstood the entire concept of culture, and actually this is all there is: juice. Mops. Pasties. PVC. CDJs. Nerve damage from drug-induced panic attacks. Is this what there is? The bathrooms and all the drains on the floor keep flooding and the heat is mounting when about a hundred people pack into the basement. Everybody takes off their shirts and I start wringing a rag of ice water down the back of my neck. In the supply closet, I see the jug: "swamp juice," but with the heat and the flooding drains and all the dance-sweat, this thick fog is only partially intentional. One of the cuter bartenders is shirtless and, blind, I stumble right into him. I feel like I'm going to asphyxiate. He says: *somebody threw up in the handwashing sink.* A vocal sample from a drum-and-bass track demands: JUNGLE IS MASSIVE.

I miss my tiny room, with all my bikini tops hung up drying with lime and blue curaçao. Cash tips all over the floor and dime bags piling up in a jewelry box. What if this is it. What if I'm going to lose my hearing. What if I'm going to get mouth cancer from cigarettes. What if this club that just opened closes at some point and everybody was too drunk to remember it and everybody forgets. What if everything goes down the drain. Or, what if nothing goes down the drain. What if this is just a flood. Or is it just summer and this is the place where I am, like last summer but with longer hair and better clothes.

I have to have become *something*, right? Misunderstanding "culture," all the club kids are actually advertisements for a dreamlike past. This is glamor: you take a past you didn't know—that didn't exist—and you go ahead and sell it to the future. There's no side effects, as far as I know. Maybe my crush on the model is a similar misunderstanding: some schizophrenic misfire of fashion advertising, where I want to catch a good price; where I want want want. After work it's five in the morning. I'm at another club, blasted out of my mind in latex I feel his hands and I'm kissing him—*I'm actually kissing him!*—and he says *we can't have sex right now I'm really high.* Ha ha—what?

Later, the sun rises over a brownstone in Bed-Stuy where I am apparently attending a sex party. A queer kink play party, whatever. The older artist takes a break from making out with a topless girl to say, *Zoey! You made it!* And I feel as though I've done something wrong. I've arrived too late, and I catch the last of it, which in this situation feels like a late-middle, and I catch it again like a late-night cartoon, watching shapes and colors move—watching, again in some strangely antiseptic voyeuristic streak—three floors of people fucking. I decide I'll wait here an hour until the diner on the corner opens because, Dear Reader, I have no other place to stay.

Reality is like that inside mythic New York, liquid bordering on cartoon, here in this ornamental George Jetson-ass place. I'm wondering if glamor is for others always, always to be devoured, to be sold alongside another negroni, feeling, and believing that this is a type of labor. Like being a girl. I don't take any of my clothes off. I taste blood on my lips, bitten raw by the model. I smoke a cigarette on the roof.

Like smoking a cigarette behind the bar, my bar, ashing it onto the floor, feeling the room go in circles, letting the fog let up. This is my favorite feeling: the pinks, the blues and greens and reds of the night's light all gone, the drinks and vomit down the drain all gone, clear water white bar Windex. I clean the bar like concealing a crime. The crime of my life.

One time I have this dream where sitting in the kitchen my father asks me, *are you on hard drugs?* In 1979, Kathy Acker says, *I want more and more horrible disaster in New York cause I desperately want to see that new thing that is going to happen this year.* In the kitchen I say, *no, I just like to watch.* In real life, Ana says, *You remember the dialogue from your dreams? I only remember colors, shapes and light.*

We Can All Live in This House

Destiny Brundidge

1.

One of the first times I attended *Soul Summit* was at Restoration Plaza in 2016, behind the Applebee's on Fulton Ave. I had taken shrooms and went alone. I didn't run into anyone I knew. The crowd was so very very Black. It was the first time I had seen a collective of Black rave *elders*. Aunties were set up in picnic chairs around the perimeter, and small children were running around them.

The sound system echoed soulfully around the plaza. I felt the bass in my lungs. Melodic bass, it was familiar to me but unnameable, like jazz. The shrooms were making me look at everyone in the eye, or maybe I was just catching eyes because it was a place where I was truly seen. It felt glorious, to be held in a gaze like that. The gaze of people who held me familially, lovingly, but couldn't name me.

It was during the day, as all *Soul Summits* are, with the sunlight sanctifying the dancefloor. Everyone who wanted to dance had room. Because I went alone, I wasn't burdened with socializing. I was able to dance in a way I hadn't usually. That feeling of floating on the shrooms, a slip in the beat I was grateful for. Some of the uniform, monotonous banging bass of what music in underground raving was becoming had been wearing me out. There is not much movement that a strict 4/4 beat can get out of me besides a two-step. With more, there is more my feet can do.

My brown crinkle poly shirt got sweaty, and I was grateful. Mostly everyone I saw was Black, as am I. Everyone knows that feeling when they are at home, when they are amongst their people, their family. The intestines relax. Your mood calms beneath everyone's warmth and smiles. Heart open, I roamed around both dance-floors, catching incredible vibes, and watching some of the best dancers I had seen in public. This was *house*.

Soul Summit was founded by DJs Sadiq Bellamy, Tabu, and Jeff Mendoza. It has been ongoing in Brooklyn for just over twenty years. Its location moves around a bit, but Fort Greene is its home. The way people dance there: really moving all limbs, advanced footwork, spinning, and jumping. Dance circles open up sporadi-cally, but you can usually find the best dancers closer to the ven-dors behind the DJ booth, where there is more space. The drum circle usually situates itself at the rear of the dancefloor, and auton-omous whistles blow throughout the crowd. Cheerful bootleggers worm throughout the festival selling nutcrackers, and if you ask them for water, they might laugh at you, full of mischief.

Soul Summit is so synonymous with Brooklyn summers that the idea has osmosed itself into my consciousness. I name 2016 as the year I first went to *Soul Summit*, but I have earlier, more dis-tant memories of being in a park, walking past a row of aunties in folding chairs while house music blared, brushing past drum circles and a dancing crowd. Maybe it was 2010, my first summer in New York City. But I had no clue where I was at any given time my first year in New York. I was too fresh out of the Black bubble I grew up in to appreciate the scenes of familiarity, to seek out the warmth of my people and the comforting timbre of our voices.

Ever since that time, I make a point to go to *Soul Summit* at least once every summer. Something shifts at Fort Greene park when it is happening. I went twice this summer. The first time, it was pouring rain. The crowd still thumped with glee and revelry. I left feeling cleansed. I welled with tears, welcoming the rain with outstretched arms while "Another Star" by Stevie Wonder played—the song that always (always?) closes *Soul Summit.*

There's something so satisfactory for a Black person to be surrounded by other Black people who are healthy, living, thriving, and joyous. If you are Black, you know what I mean. There's a warming clarity. How rare it is to be in a crowd of your own in peace and love, not shaded by grief, poverty, or the aggression and depravity that comes with captivity. While walking with my friends searching for the nearest bathroom that wasn't a port-a-potty, a Black man walking towards the festival turned towards us and said, "Black people are so beautiful." You may find yourself or hear others saying such remarks. "Wow, look at us!", "Black people so fine," or "My people!!" I think that moments like this, of collective self-recognition, are felt by everyone in the vicinity. Even if you aren't Black, it must be nice to see us happy and beautiful, too. Even if just for a day. That energy coats the park and spreads throughout the surrounding neighborhoods. *Soul Summit* sets the tone for all of Brooklyn on the day when it is happening.

2.

That time I went to *Soul Summit* in 2016, techno was taking over the underground scene in NYC. The music in nightlife was transitioning from "experimental club," an amorphous genre that sampled elements from a vast sonic range, from jersey to juke to ballroom, pop, industrial noise, and vocal snippets. What people were calling "the club" before was beginning to give way to "the rave." I was following the flow. I admit to missing the messier, more colorful club days, but long before the term "rave" resurfaced I had figured out that raving was something I just needed to do. I was trying to heal myself from depression, and figured that the sweaty overnight shift was crucial to my recovery. The clarity and cleanliness I felt after a purge like that, my joints lubricated after hours of movement, the safety I felt in darkness within a crowd. With no pressure to talk, I could ruminate and comb through my thoughts for hours, undisturbed and un-alone.

The reason I fell in love with raving had to do with transcendence— altered states of being that open portals to liberation breaking through the redundancy of the day to day. It has to do with procession, in both the celebratory and funerary senses. The non-place we go to repeatedly, the place that only exists in between days, that only exists when we show up. The warehouse, the dancefloor, the darkroom are intangible spaces that only appear through coordinated efforts between the organizers and the ravers. This coordination can adapt to political movements, where rave organizers can appropriate their skills to a march.

Ravers can appropriate their bodies to show up to protest. I witnessed this intimately during the New York City George Floyd protests of 2020. The spontaneity and covert conspiring needed to throw a rave—the spatial and social awareness honed after hours spent in crowds, the mutual aid and care necessary to endure through dehydration or drug use—are useful skills. The long streams of information, gossip of where to go, how it was, who and what to avoid, run just as easily toward the streets of protest. These rave behaviors were developed to evade police and surveillance, for Black, queer, and marginalized people to embody forms of liberation and authenticity prohibited in the current paradigm.

There is a struggle between the power behind dominant structures and the power behind the essential compulsions inherent to the social nature of humanity: the need to collectively burp. Or celebrate. Or scheme. Or heal. Or grieve. The rave is a way to collectively express our most ecstatic desires, and ritualistically manifest collective will is what is being discussed here. Collectivity is a substantive process, and crucial to our functioning. The special combination of resistance and liberation is what charges our form called "raving." Like how the ancient Roman historian Livy describes the Bacchanalia cult festival as a murderous instrument of conspiracy against the state.[1]

The word "rave" has origins within British language, and the UK is the place of some of the most infamous and iconic raves in known history. Lots of work has been done in recent years to remind people that the music of raves—techno, house, dnb, etc—is of Black origin, nodding toward a longer history, across the African diaspora, and by proxy every diaspora that has ever happened. Black culture (in the context of the Atlantic slave trade) has had a special role in the history of raving as a format of gathering and a practice of resistance. I know this to be true: through my fleshy memory, my sweat and pores, my feet dancing to steps I've never been taught.

I think of notorious fêtes, speakeasies, and séances held in secret. I think of processions of all kinds of movement: carnivals, funerals, and riots. Forms of ecstatic collectivity, so called "raves," have a longer and much darker history than is typically discussed. Darker as in skin tones, and as in what is hidden, as in deep underground, in shade, in secret, and dark rooms occluded by night. Special shades that provide protection for what is sacred, and precious to life. It is in this context that raving exists and thrives today. Our enactment of freedom, our play, is a rehearsal and also the execution of our autonomy, our love, our joy.

3.

The time I went to *Soul Summit* in 2016 was the day I met Jeff. Sitting on the side of the dancefloor, he complimented me on my dancing. He flirted with me by making me guess his age. He claimed to be over sixty but wouldn't tell me exactly. "The only reason why I'm not dancing is because my knees, you know, they get tight with age," he said. "But next time, when I take you out, you will see." We sat on the side and chatted. During pauses, he would scream, blow his whistle, sing along to the music. I was amused to be hit on by someone near retirement age. He seemed so familiar. We became friends.

Jeff took me around to all his raves: *Soul Summit*, *Paradise Garage Reunion*, *Shelter*, and *Clubhouse Jamboree*. He was from Queens and started going out when he was fourteen years old. "Paradise Garage was *It*," he said, screaming into my ear over sound systems between bouts of dancing. "The Loft was exclusive and mainly for the gay crowd," and "Studio 54 was for white people. Nobody really danced there anyways." Paradise Garage was utopia because everyone, EVERYONE was there. It was underground to the whole city. Race, sexuality, and class didn't matter.

He described himself at times as an underage kid running wild, as a cool kid in his early 20s pulling an all-black studded leather look, and a professional adult, sweating out his button up shirt after a day of work. When he started working on Wall Street, he would start at the Irish pubs in FiDi, and eventually make his way to the Village or Midtown. People would go out immediately after work, and it wasn't all about the looks, the way it seems looking back now. It was a lot of regular folks with two sides: daytime and nighttime.

Once, when I was with him at a *Paradise Garage Reunion* party at Elsewhere, there were these fantastic dancers, house stepping, with vogueing and breakdancing elements. It was almost gymnastic. I was absolutely enchanted. "See that?" Jeff ranted in my ear. "That's that Loft style of dancing, they take up too much space! This ain't a Loft reunion party this is a *Paradise Garage Reunion* party. They need to take that shit elsewhere! I don't like that, how they take up all the space and everyone has to form a circle around them, and ain't nobody else can dance unless they get hit in the face!"

Jeff was *furious*. I chuckled. I had gotten used to Jeff's fluctuating temper. Once at Output (which died in 2018), we were dancing together in the center on the main floor, and a group of white couples excitedly pushed through the crowd. They pushed Jeff right out of the way. I caught his rage just in time before it blew all over these strangers. The white couples turned around looking confused, meeting Jeff's eyes blazing with fury as I dragged him away.

"These white people, they just try to walk right through you. And they can't even dance on beat," he ranted. "They don't know where they are, they just want to be at the center of this thing they see that has history and looks cool. But they know nothing, they're not connected, they don't even see people. It's the same thing like this gentrification," but of his scene, of his family. They come into an already formed and thriving situation, take over and threaten to kick the earlier generation out. And it wasn't just about "white people." The scene ultimately is about acceptance and unity, but this specific kind of entitlement from this younger generation—"they don't know where they are, and don't care," he said.

When I asked him about *Soul Summit*, he said he really liked that party, but admitted it was being taken over by young white people. When it's in the park during the summer, it's good but it gets crowded. When it's at other places (like Nowadays) other times of year, the crowd gets too white, and some of the spirit gets lost. He loves *Shelter* and *Paradise Garage Reunion* because there are more people and songs he knows, more familiarity, more memories. But according to him, all of it— *Shelter*, *Soul Summit*, *PGR*—was a part of a revival moment that started in the late '90s, early 2000s, and none of it has the energy of the original, of course.

The burnout of Jeff's scene generation started in the late '80s. They dominated NYC for nearly two decades, but the burnout corresponds with a natural turnover that comes with life (career, spouse, and kids), and the AIDS crisis. He talked about how many people were lost to AIDS, and how people were starting to get together in the late '90s for remembrance parties, to commemorate those who passed away. Sometime after *Shelter* closed, the club's founder Timmy Regisford started throwing raves in different locations. Then the *Paradise Garage Reunion* parties started, which brought out people from the original scene. This house music revival scene was born.

Hanging out with Jeff gave me a real education. Up to meeting him, I listened to hip hop, contemporary club, and a lot of funk, fusion, and modal jazz, but I fell off hard between the years 1980 and 1989. I considered myself a student of African American Music Studies, without ever going to school, but there were huge deficits in my listening history. After going with Jeff to his raves, I finally began to understand how the same people who raved to disco went on to create and enjoy techno. I made the connection between the Black music I listened to, and the disembodied techno rhythms that were starting to dominate the city. Jeff explained to me that it's not all about the voiceless beat instrumentals; that disembodied sound came from somewhere, and to restrict the mix just to the beat misses the musicians, lyrics, and powerful singers—the important origins of house music. Now I began to more clearly hear the evolution of the music, from funk and jazz, to disco to house to techno.

House music and techno are often discussed today as if they are rivals. Other times, the genres are discussed as if they are polarities of a Janus face: two faces on a head that sees in all directions. House music looks toward the past, looping disco faves into melodic echoes and familiar breakbeats, whereas techno looks toward the future, a space sanctified by the erasure of race, gender, and emotional human flamboyance. When disco was first electrified in the '70s, its incessant bassline awoke the giant monster, and it was house's eyes that opened first, its face turning for wider views. Soon after, its face split, to view beyond the angels of its neck, spawning techno, its darksided twin. Many faces fanned out from there, to create the multitude of dance music genres that we know and love today—acid, jungle, dubstep etc.

Yet house music defiantly holds the memory of Black music, squarely looking at the people: gay, feminine and free. A good house music set maintains a steady beat with a swing and heavy bass on the twos that the pelvis can keep up with, reminiscent of the iconic disco break. It's indiscriminate in including vocals calling to Loleatta Halloway, or back even further to spirituals and gospels that sing for pain and liberation. A single set can span three or four decades of music, recalling history while signaling loudly toward the future, anticipating the arrival of more children.

4.

Remembering is revisiting which is ultimately re-creating once again. What is legacy, if not the reassembly of past conditions to be experienced again and again in the present? To return, by reassembling ourselves, we blow pockets in time, air bubbles for us to breathe. Each breath of life expands our space, a space defined more by our unity than by location and time. To go once is to never forget, to go again is to never leave. To create definitions of unity is paramount to our ability to survive. How do we re-assemble? How do we find each other in the noise?[2]

This past summer, a friend of mine who wasn't able to come to one of the *Soul Summits* at Fort Greene texted me after asking me if the party had fully turned into a majority-white event. She had seen stories on Instagram. There were barely any Black people in the crowd she saw. White attendees weren't yet a majority, but had completely centered themselves on the main floor. Right before my cherished memory in the rain, a white women leading a train of her friends tried to push past me to get to the center of the floor. I guess she assumed a space would open up for her. Instead, her push almost separated me from my friend, whom I grabbed close.

Last year at the park, I had become psychedelically incensed by a human chain of white gays, creating a fleshy, impassable block right at the center dancefloor. "This isn't Basement!!" I screamed in a shroom-fueled tirade. I ranted to my friends, who all stared at me in a silence both amused and solemn. We sat in the park after the festival, lightning bugs tinkling around us in the dark.

The magic of the day wouldn't wear off for at least another thirty-six hours, despite my emotional disturbance. I was angered because a phenomenon I experienced in nightlife was happening at a day-time party I went to for solace, for familiarity, and for remembrance: being pushed off the floor by a muscle-gay orgy. I boiled at the thought of witchy Black aunties who fanned themselves and any-one standing near them being stepped on by white men obliv-ious to anyone besides each other and their own pleasure. Did they know where they were? Here at this space created by the very Black elders that structured the precursor to the nightlife they experience today, could they decenter themselves?

At both *Soul Summit* Fort Greene events I was able to attend this summer, the floors were so packed it was almost impossible to move at all. Jeff and I texted in hopes that we would run into each other, but I couldn't find him. Sorry I didn't get to see you," was all he texted after.

As a Black person, it feels really eerie seeing our culture without our people. It's like seeing a body without its head, and you're the head. It comes with the panic and the indignation of feeling murdered. The anger and frustration of being victimized, having been overwhelmed by your attacker. All of this emotion, but in a muffled, almost sedated state. You may find yourself laughing at the absurdity.

Dying people laugh, too. This is a bit how I felt attending the *Soul Summit* at Nowadays. It is a collaboration with *Mister Sunday*, so, it's really not a measure of the core community of *Soul Summit*. The entry fee for Nowadays is $30, a deviation from the usual free, open air format of *Soul Summit*. Since capitalism is the current paradigm, I don't have a problem with this. I'm glad that *Soul Summit* has some means to generate capital to sustain its space. But the price (and location) deters its core audience, and exposes the event to a crowd that shifts the demographics of the party at other times of the year. There were a few Black elders there, full of joy and exuberance as usual, but the majority of the crowd was of college-aged white kids with that sort of smoothed face, uncomplicated sheen.

It was the day after the attack on Israeli citizens by Hamas militants, and the beginning of the horrific retaliatory genocidal bombardment onto the people of Gaza. My attention split between my reality and the ongoing violence. I eagerly looked to the Black elders there for eye contact to connect and ground myself, and I did magnetize briefly to an uncle, who complimented me on my head scarf.

"You know that's how they wear it in other cultures!" Yes, I knew, but I appreciated this little moment of familiarity, in that way of getting "schooled" by an elder, and the subtle nod towards Islam. The rest of the evening, I spent sort of dazed, half-present. Headless, my consciousness seeped out to other times and spaces, as if diluted in a sea. My body, invisibilized, treaded on and pushed aside. I wondered if I was really there.

Looking at *Soul Summit* documentation on YouTube, the turn is really apparent. In 2010, the crowd is majority-Black and there is a lot more room to dance. By 2023, there are stills where you can only count a few Black faces, and the crowd is so dense people can barely move. In a YouTube interview, co-founder Sadiq Bellamy describes attempts to shut down the party by gentrifiers new to the neighborhood. He explains how the event has been restricted in Fort Greene Park, going from ten events a summer down to two. "*Soul Summit* preceded the very people that moved in." It seems the survival of the party is contingent on newcomers becoming aware of the history of this space, and the context for this tradition.

Considering the reality of rave culture and nightlife today, I ask (mostly white) newcomers: Is it so necessary to create a white mass at the center of this event? Maybe use some spatial awareness for where you situate yourself on the dancefloor. Try dancing around the perimeter, or set up a little picnic on the lawn with friends to enjoy the music. Get cruised by a Black daddy by the monument or support one of the vendors tabling around the park. Maybe, just walk around and simply observe this unique and precious instant of Black community and love.

Returning sustains memory; repetitive return creates the contour of culture and the dimensions of a people. There's an obvious linkage of the shifting demographics of *Soul Summit* to the colonial white supremacist project that displaces people, again and again. But another theme that keeps coming up for me in this moment is *context*. To know context, specifically your context, is to understand your relationship to place and everyone around you. Because the goal isn't to segregate ourselves from one another and erect walls. Circulation is essential to the living. We must see and know one another, and bear witness to all life. We get to know ourselves better through our differences, and with the awareness of the boundaries that define I from other. Without context, we will destroy the landscape and overpower memory with oblivion.

A Berlin Welcome
Frankie Wiener

I arrive in Berlin Thursday evening. This is my first time in this city, my first time solo traveling, my first time leaving the country since I was eighteen, my first time being away from home for this long. Shortly after getting in, I head to a small party at a friend's apartment organized to welcome me. Ten or twelve friends are there and it feels warm. It is clear that I am loved.

Friday night comes and I get dressed at my place for *Gegen*, following a local friend's advice of "less is more."

Four of us head over together. With the help of the guestlist line, we are inside KitKat in a few minutes. Signs in the entrance read "Nudity is a personal choice" and we are told to check our phones along with our bags and clothing. All I keep with me is what I can hold in my socks: cash, drugs, two condoms. A friend with a bag holds my other party essentials: cigarettes, poppers, a small bottle of lube, more condoms just in case. I spend the first thirty minutes exploring the multiple large dancefloors, black-lit psychedelic hallways, semi-outdoor pool area, four or five bars, endless beds and nooks to fuck in, and the mesmerizing room on the lower level filled with medical beds and equipment. I promise myself I will make good use of that space before my evening is over.

The dancefloors are full early and I am quickly consumed by the energy of the largest one, on the main floor. Everyone is hot, gorgeously adorned with intricate fetish wear, and slicked with sweat from the dense summer heat. I navigate my way onto a platform at the front right of the DJ booth. The bass thumps inside me. I let my eyes wander and my hips and knees get directed by the music. I scan the floor and recognize not a single person in my view. I cannot recall the last time this statement was true. I think about how freeing it is to feel momentarily anonymous, not a dancefloor fixture like I am at home in New York. To be just another sweaty body, to marvel at everyone's beauty and not feel the need to avert my eyes. I let the freedom sink in. I feel seen but not surveilled.

Around 5 a.m. I'm sitting near the pool taking a break from dancing. I've found my friends. I am drinking a coffee with Bailey's and notice someone staring at me, hard. He does not avert his eyes when I look up. Back home, this might be considered creepy—leering, even—but here in this moment, he appears hungry. Earlier, a friend had told me that direct eye contact as a means of saying "I want to fuck" is more acceptable here. As I experience it for the first time, a large part of me appreciates the direct communication. I look again, letting my eyes linger, and find him sexy. I put aside my discomfort with this dance and we stare directly at each other for a minute or so, scanning one another's bodies and dispositions. He gets up and comes to sit beside me. We exchange greetings, but his primary language is Portuguese, so words are brief. Soon his hand is on my thigh, then his tongue in my mouth, then I'm pulled onto his lap. I feel how eager he is and my excitement meets my anxiety as I wonder to myself what he thinks he knows about me. As if reading my mind, he asks me, "Are you uhhhh. . . into trans?" I simultaneously cringe and laugh a bit with relief. I remind myself that English is not his first language and choose not to judge his phrasing. I nod. "I am trans, if that's what you're asking." He smiles as he looks at me, tight-gripped hands grabbing and rubbing down my thighs. The anxiety still lingers as I leave certain details unsaid. I allow myself to feel it.

I lead him to a caged bed nook just off the main dancefloor to get what we both crave. I'm back on top of him, one hand in his little pleather shorts teasing his cock and the other planted firmly on his chest, when I feel the sudden need to disclose clearly that I have a pussy. He raises his eyebrows and responds "Really? Wow. Okay." I realize I haven't gotten this far into a hookup with a stranger without direct disclosure since the beginning of my transition more than five years ago. I think about how exhilarating it feels to push my mind's limits, but also sit with the reality of risk when choosing my liberation over my safety.

He pushes me on my back and consumes me, his body weight holding me down as he fills me up. I decide I deserve pleasure without explanation. He instructs me to flip over again, this time on all fours, and fucks me with my face pressed against the bars of the caged wall, giving me a direct view of the dancefloor. I decide to stop thinking and sink into a deeper intoxicated state from the drugs and the music and the dick pounding any last thoughts out of my brain. We're being watched and I lean into my exhibitionism. He pulls me back against him with a hand around my throat and the other around my waist and kisses me like he needs it. The power of my freedom adds to my pleasure.

We finish up and dance together for a moment before I wander off. I play a bit with others. Dance more. Talk to friends. Meet new people in overcrowded bathroom stalls. Get yelled at by a bathroom attendant for overcrowding a bathroom stall. I learn how Berliners do their drugs. I've recently found myself bored of the substances in my rotation at home. Ketamine has left me feeling disconnected and the psychedelics most accessible to me a bit too unpredictable. Here my friends' regular go-tos are drugs I'm less familiar with: mephedrone, speed, 2C-B. I decide to trust them and indulge. They make me feel powerful, present and sexy. A noticeable contrast.

A group of cute girls sit by the pool and one smiles at me as I'm passing, so I ask to join them. I talk to several, but one in particular piques my interest. She tells me she was watching me on the floor earlier and thought the way I danced was sexy. She tells me I seem free. We flirt and kiss, tenderly at first, then with fervor. A few minutes later her legs are propped up in a gyno exam chair in the medical room, my fingers inside two of her holes, fulfilling my earlier promise to myself about using this space. She is aggressive and hungry, like me. We fight for power, ravenous and sweaty, and I succumb to her strength and once again feel consumed. I let her have me however she wants. She leans into her sadism, testing me, but I am not new to pushing my body past what my mind thinks it can take. When the party's over at 10 a.m. I take her home with me.

My alarm wakes me up at 8 a.m. Sunday morning after five hours of sleep. Shortly after, my calendar app sends me a notification that simply reads, "Klubnacht." I try to hold back any expectations, but while taking a hot shower, I do set intentions: I want to dance hard and long. I want to fuck. I want an espresso martini. I want to close it out.

I pick my outfit carefully, knowing I want to feel as free as possible. Mostly fishnet. Lots of chains and hardware. Easy access. I arrive outside Berghain at 10 a.m. and wait for my friend. A beefy leather-clad man comes up to me and tells me in half-German, half-English that he saw me play in the downstairs room at KitKat on Friday. I laugh and accept my hypervisibility. I cannot both put on a show and expect to be anonymous.

My friend arrives. There is no line, and the bouncer waves us in with a nod and smile. It's slow and there's abundant time to get settled in these new surroundings. I walk up the long wide concrete staircase to the main dancefloor and marvel at how huge and dramatic the space is. I admire the seemingly hundred-foot ceilings, the beautiful glass-paneled windows that separate the dancefloor from the right side bar, and the several large visible staircases to floors I've yet to see. I explore how the soundsystem feels in my body from different places on the main dancefloor as I stare upwards in awe, sporadic beams of light exposing the faces of dancers around me. Just like back home, I prefer front left.

I find a cubby near the Panorama Bar bathrooms. I look up while smoking a cigarette and notice the dynamic purple and blue lighting reflected onto each wall. Large, triangular, numbered pieces of metal are attached to the ceiling above my head. I assume they are remnants of this building's past as a thermal power plant, but at this moment, they are just little details that keep my mind busy while I smoke. I notice the number eighteen is visible from my seat—my lucky number, the Hebrew numerological equivalent for the word *chai*, meaning life, living, life force. It is the Hebrew word shouted over drinks—*l'chaim,* to life, an invocation of really and truly being *alive.* It feels like a sign, a reminder to not take my beautiful, complex, sacred life for granted. This becomes my chosen break spot.

I take my first venture into the darkroom with a friend. Almost instantly I feel an anonymous touch graze me and allow an unseen figure to feel me up for a moment, but quickly brush the hand off. I prefer to be able to see the people I fuck and decide to do my cruising where that is possible. I go get a smoothie. I meet friends of friends in bathroom lines. I pause to thank myself and the powers that have put me here, in this body in this place at this moment, for allowing me the experiences of pleasure and perseverance that make life worth living. I settle in for the long haul.

Gabrielle Kwarteng is playing in the Garten and her set is cunty as fuck. It's a hot afternoon, around ninety degrees, and I take abundant breaks to drink water straight from the faucet. I dance hard and loud, throwing my hips and sending my hands in circles as high in the air as I can reach, struck by how queer and joyous this dancefloor is. A friend from home leans in and says "This feels so New York." He is right.

Night comes and energy shifts. Norman Nodge begins a beautiful, pounding, powerful set on the main floor. I dance what feels like the hardest I ever have (I say this once every few months). I release deep, justified anger that's lived in my body far too long, letting the music and the drugs command my muscles and joints and nerves as I lean deep into my hedonism. I keep asking myself "What do you *want?*" Whatever the answer, I let myself have it, trusting I can take it.

As the night progresses I trust my body deeper and deeper. I contemplate how there are few things in this world that satisfy me as much as proving to myself that I am stronger than my brain wants me to believe, and soaking up the gifts I receive when I push just a bit further than I think I can take. This mindset is how I have built everything I have and love. I satisfy the intentions I'd made earlier in the shower, indulging in the most delicious, smooth, frothy espresso martini I've ever had, at 6 a.m., with a boy I want. Afterwards, the two of us go to the bathroom to re-up and it is his turn to ask: "What do you want?" I look him in the face and tell him I want to fuck him.

We negotiate where this will happen: I offer front left on the main dancefloor but he seems more enthused about the darkroom. I accept. He tells me to lead and I don't hesitate. I ask him how he likes to be handled. He replies, "firmly." We stay close enough to the entrance that we are not fully hidden in the dark void. I can see the expression on his face as I penetrate him for the first time, and the expressions of the onlookers who we have already drawn in. I feel the subwoofers' vibrations in my body through the floor as I kneel on one knee for leverage. With my fingers inside him I turn my head for just a moment and revel in the delight of how many faggots have gathered around, jerking off, watching two transsexuals fuck. My body is already exhausted but I push a little more, giving the boy all I think he can take. We finish our business a little before 8 a.m.—just enough time to release the remains of my soul and gratitude onto the dancefloor for Barker's close. I'm near loved ones from home and more than anything, I am sunk deep into the truth of my liberation and self-knowledge.

I make it back to my sublet, take a long, hot, extremely necessary bath, nap for a few hours, and spend the afternoon at a nude spa for the very first time to soothe a bit of the ache in my body. My mind is opening to what I am capable of, what I deserve, and what I do not need to hold myself back from. The rave often gives me this gift of introspection. Even with all the work I have done, I still have a lot to learn about myself. I feel sore, open to receive, and freer than I had before.

Born-again Freak
cranberry thunderfunk

Five a.m. Front-right. Dripping head to toe. A friend turns to me and asks, "Were you always a freak? Or were you born-again?"

It's an easy question. My life couldn't have started out further from the rave.

I am the son of a preacher, raised in a Christian fundamentalist sect sometimes known as the "frozen chosen." "Chosen" due to our fatalist doctrine, "frozen" because we did not move during Sunday church services. That meant no clapping—not with the music, not for the musicians. No spontaneous outbursts, no chanting or cheering, no "amens" or "hallelujahs." No swaying, no hands in the air and of *course, obviously,* most *certainly*—no dancing.

Such quaint expressions would draw attention to us and that would be stealing glory away from a jealous and silent god. We believed the best way to worship the all-powerful, all-knowing creator of the infinite universe was by sitting still, hands folded neatly in lap. Because our worship was motionless, we saw no need for percussion—who needs drums when god gave us the metronome?

Rhythm and groove were distractions from the pursuit of technical precision. We didn't *play* the violin, we *labored* over the violin for perfection, in fear of sinful mistakes.

At home, our musical diet was guided by the same values. We mostly listened to classical or perhaps the latest barn-burners out of the Christian contemporary industry, like Jars Of Clay or DC Talk. Any secular sounds were restricted to the soft, ambiguous, unthreatening likes of Enya and Yanni. Our music was preparation for a quiet, atomized life, destined for cubicles and cul-de-sac suburbia. This was the protestant work ethic in action, where pleasure is distraction, cleanliness is godliness, and silence is golden. In every way, the opposite of the club. Yet that is the first and only place where I found spiritual communion.

It was Monday night at Bossa Nova Civic Club. I came out on a whim and didn't think I would stay long. The club was sparsely filled, the floor was sticky from last night's party, the lights had been repeating the same inert purple pattern all night, and drunk tourists kept asking me for K. In other words: a typical weeknight at Bossa—except that AceMo was on the decks. That was all that mattered. In this most dubious of settings, under the guidance of an expert dancefloor composer, I learned that god does speak. You just need some big fucking subwoofers to hear it.

The divine conversation of the dancefloor does not take place in such a paltry language as English, with the everyday violence of its grammar and syntax. The music teaches me how to speak with more than just my tongue, to use all of my body's six hundred muscles to embrace the full spectrum of sound.

It starts with hips and shoulders for the kick drum. Add knees and toes for the snare, some fingers for the hi-hat, then wrists and elbows for the melody. Time and repetition bring momentum; with each phrase, my trust in the music builds alongside trust in myself. I can feel the floor opening up around me; I am taking space. I can trip without falling; there are no mistakes. I am asymmetrical; my left can move freely from my right. I am gliding between the tourists with their concrete feet. I am dodging the boy carrying four beers. I am talking to god in the corner of Bossa on a Monday night.

I spent the first twenty years of my life, thousands of hours, in prayer and study, chasing after the faintest whisper of spiritual engagement, to no avail. I had always imagined spiritual experiences as a visitation, a vision, a possession, or perhaps something totally out-of-body. This was the opposite: it was a re-embodiment, a joyous reunion with my own flesh and bone after a lifetime of estrangement. I was made whole, and without shame. In the face of such an enormous blessing, my body's sole purpose was to express my gratitude and celebrate this sonic gift. In return, I received the baptism of sweat. If the club is my church, sweat is my holy water.

At home, I began exploring the religious history of dance. From Barbara Ehrenreich's *Dancing in the Streets*, I learned that once upon a time, Anglo-European Christianity—by which I mean white Christianity—was a danced religion. The history of the Catholic church through the Middle Ages is littered with missives from cardinals and bishops, chastising their congregations for outbursts of dancing mid-service. Sitting in church may not have been an option at all; pews were often a limited luxury reserved for the wealthy, land-owning churchgoers. Bibles were rare and most people were illiterate anyway, so their everyday spirituality was first and foremost a physical, communal experience. By contrast, the church of my childhood is a relatively recent phenomenon. But I'm sure the medieval papacy would regard the "frozen chosen" with approval.

Learning this history felt like I had uncovered my own personal Da Vinci Code: an enormous conspiracy, an intergenerational psyop to separate the soul from the body for the sake of more efficient economic subjugation. If this project has its roots in church dogma, today it finds an institutional home in technology. Our world wants us to hate our bodies, to feel insufficient and dissatisfied, to become disconnected and broken. The club may not always be a sanctuary from this oppression, but more than anywhere else I know, it offers the opportunity to take a stand.

The dancefloor is where I go to reclaim my humanity against the imperialist campaign of disembodiment. This is where I practice the truth that I am not a brain in a jar or a soul in a cage. I am my body, my body is me, and there is no room for shame when the music is this good.

Five a.m. Front-right. Dripping head to toe. I am a born-again freak.

Sloop, or How I Learned to Shut Up and Start Dancing

Alice Hines

Dear X, I'm writing to introduce myself. I'm a journalist working on a story. It's about embryo testing. It's about Covid vaccines. It's about this guy who eats goat testicles on TikTok. I'm seeking to understand the situation with its many layers of nuance. My project is still in early stages, but I'm convinced that no dive into this topic would be complete without you. Would you be available for a call? Thank you for finding the time. Can you say that again, but more casually, like you're talking to a friend?

I go on like that most days. Coaxing, provoking, sympathizing, performing interest. Voiceovers. Social headlines. Scripts. Narratives. I spend three years on a story and then distill it into a five-minute segment for a local news anchor, and then I do that twenty more times.

Words feel like the best way to connect with other people, organize the messiness of experience. I can create patterns from noise, give names to feelings. Lying awake and hearing maybe-imaginary sounds? That's insomnia. Using at least five drugs…simultaneously? Polypharmacy. "Pins and needles" gave me a relief at age eight that I still remember, because it suggested my legs weren't actually going to fall off. Later, I become fluent in useful short-hands for the difficult-to-describe, like ineffable, problematic, or vibe.

Finding the right words feels like being in control, even when the opposite is true. Once, there was sex that didn't make sense, which felt abject, that I didn't think I wanted. I realized later what that was called. It was comforting to know that even the worst things could be commiserated.

Words are empowering and then sometimes they are exhausting. Have you ever stared too long at a sentence on a screen? It becomes unfamiliar and meaningless, like a smudge. Narrating could make my mouth dry and my chest tight. It's creeping up on me that my tools for interacting with the world are arbitrary metaphors, their shapes and sounds never exactly corresponding to what I mean. Words are the keys to experience. They are also the noisy gatekeepers of experience. I want to throw the key away, or snort something off of it. People talk about dissociating. Could I dearticulate?

On a rainy Friday night in Brooklyn, I walk into a warehouse party where my friend is playing. I'm early, and I sit with my friend behind the booth. We talk about stuff that feels frivolous and fun, like logos and movies. He plays some 1990s chillout tracks, and we smoke a joint. The words in my head turn into beats. Delete. Rewrite. Delete. Rewrite. Delete. Rewrite. Delete. Rewrite. They repeat until they stop being words at all. If I stay out long enough this weekend, I'll hear music in the dishwasher on Monday.

Later, I head to a club. My friends aren't here yet, so I find a spot near the fog machine and dance with my eyes closed. The smell is a trigger. So is the strobe, other people's sweat, and the music, although that's the hardest part to describe. People use phrases like acid house, or psychedelic techno, or polyrhythmic. Fuck it, why not polypharmarhythmic? But the truth is that the music is a cipher. You can project metaphors onto it, or not.

Abstraction is a property of most music, not just electronic. I read that sound travels almost five times as fast across human tissue as it does through air. It's fitting that these waveforms can pull the levers of our emotions while bypassing our thoughts. There's a quote I like from the psychologist and pianist Ruth Herbert, about how her internal experience of listening to music is chameleonic. "At any time," she writes, "I might find myself 'wallowing' in the sound, exposed to unbidden imagery, narratives, associations and memories, notice myself analyzing aspects of the music, experience my surroundings slightly differently—or even forget the very presence of music."

Here on the dancefloor, I feel like my body is part of the sound wave. Vibrating flesh. A name for this unutterable feeling occurs to me. It's Sloop. S-L-DOUBLE-O-P. Riff on the number of O's. Sloop. Slooooop. Sloop! I connect with Sloop again later, during sex. I typically love dirty talk and name calling, but I'm sick of all the usual suspects. My erotic mind has been taken over by power structures and their henchman, language. I am searching for something else, and Sloop bubbles up out of my subconscious. While my physical body bears labels—girl, thin, white—as Sloop, I'm sentient slime.

I return to Sloop periodically on the dancefloor. I can find my way there when I feel a bassline and it subtly vibrates the micro hairs on my arm, or creates friction between shirt and skin. Sloop doesn't think—we move. When I am Sloop, and when we become Sloop, our dance moves have no meaning. We dance like we have no bones. We know the words to tracks with no words.

I open my eyes. I look at a disco ball. It's spinning continuously, light and shadow contained in its sphere. I think I see a piece of myself in one of its fragments, but I can't be sure whether it's actually someone else, and then it's gone.

Four Folk Tales

Simon Wu

The Lovers

I found myself in a part of town I'd never seen before, on the other side of the city center, closer to the water but further from where I was staying.

The first time I visited this place I was with my mother, and she told me about a man-made lake at its center. We were sitting in traffic, helplessly sweating, as a hot afternoon fog drifted over the road. She said she went on dates there in high school, away from her parents, and that they called it Lover's Lake at the time, but she was sure it had a much more official name somewhere. The lake was infamous because many young people had drowned within its shores on drunken escapades, thinking it much shallower than it actually was. From the road all you could see was the flowering trees around the perimeter, their boughs burdened with blooms with a raised walkway around the lake, as if the road was hunching its shoulders up in a question.

I was meeting my friend, the Fox, at a market called The General's Market, a former colonial building that had been repurposed into an open-air bazaar after a fire rendered many of its rooms unusable. There was a physical comedy to the place, in the way of many architectures that are built for one thing and used for another. Administrators, now hawkers, were bitter and territorial over their wares. On the plane back to the city, just a few days later, I'd remember just the smell of smoke and turmeric.

My friend was already busy haggling. He was introduced to me as someone who was from *here*, who went to high school *here* and lived *here,* while I was mostly from *there* with only some flavoring of *here*.

I took a walk to give him some space. Down the street, past a chain-link fence, I could see a squat grey warehouse where the Fox and I would go dancing later tonight. We had been there last night as well, deep into the morning, and I remembered that somewhere near sunrise, as the light had thrown itself through the windows, I had been struck with the thought that every place that had Fog— every dancefloor, every club, in every city and town and nation where there was a machine that could make Fog thick enough that you could not see your hands in front of your face—was actually the same place, and they were connected to each other in a vast network of rooms and inlets that you could visit simply by entering your local discothèque. You would find your past and future lovers there; your past and future selves, enemies and mothers, homes and vacations, as well as lakes and mountains to wander through. It was your favorite place and the place you avoided at all costs. It was different every time but also always the same.

At the corner, where the cab drivers loitered, a burnt tree of a man sat next to a cage filled with birds, seemingly more birds than I had ever seen in my life, chirping frantically. They looked like a swarm of bees but less menacing and more soothing, as if their beaks might administer a balm rather than a poison. I watched two particularly small sparrows. One with a blue spot on its head, the other all white, pecking at the corner.

"You can pay a couple coins and free some of them, if you'd like," my friend suggested by way of greeting.

"I've never seen anything like this," I said, giving him a hug.

"It's pretty common here. You pay to release some sparrows, and it's good karma. People who have something they need to let go."

I asked if I could free two birds specifically and the vendor said that he would try, so I gestured to the two that had been pecking at the corner earlier, hoping that I could reward their cunning. He reached his hand in the swarm and then mumbled something inaudibly.

"He says one of them is already dead," my friend said. "You want to free them anyways?"

"That's all right," I told the vendor, and he grabbed the other one and a new one from the top and held them out for me to hold. Their small, frantic bodies buzzed in my hands. I held them long enough to feel that I was their jailer, and then I threw them up above my head, where they evaporated.

The Rabbit

I think that in a past life I was a Rabbit that lived in a forest. A big green forest with vales and valleys and meadows, where the sky was blue and vaulted, and the Fog from the mountains was thick enough that you could not see your hands in front of your face. I lived there with my friends the fox and the monkey.

One day a celestial being came to test our loyalty to him. He came down from the sky disguised as a beggar and asked each of us to bring him something to eat. Generous as we were, we set out to honor the poor being's request. The Fox, cunning and agile, returned with a fish. The Monkey, intelligent and nimble, returned with a banana. As a small and more limited animal, I, the Rabbit, could only bring back grass. Ashamed by my feeble offering, in a surge of heroic conviction, I ignited the grass. I watched the flames tear orange rips into the black night. I dipped a paw and felt it singe. In a flash of certainty, like a stone falling into a well, I closed my eyes and stepped into the orange rips, and let it coat my throat and singe my eyes, the smoke so thick that I could not see my hands in front of my face. I burned.

The gesture so touched the beggar-emperor that he decided to reward me, and he sent me to the moon to become its honored guardian.

At first life on the moon was wonderful: the view was extraordinary, and the isolation comforting. I was given spacious living quarters and was able to furnish it to my liking. But it soon became strange and lonely. I found it difficult to make a home so far from where I had come. I replayed the moment when I lit the fire—the shock of smoke, the sear of the embers—over and over again and I wondered if this reserve of selflessness still resided within me, or if I had depleted it with that action, or if it had never existed within me to begin with and I had conjured it to fill another's need. How often was I prone to this kind of total dissolution? Sometimes I remembered the fire differently, like self-sublimation instead of self-destruction, a fog instead of a fire. But on my lowest days, I felt that my guardianship, given as a reward for an act of selflessness, had become a prison.

The Fox
I had not planned on having a good time.

At the warehouse, the line for the coat check curled around the block, and an enormous makeshift curtain separated the dance-floor from the bathrooms. The warehouse was usually a kids' circus, with summer camps for somersaults and backflips and children's gymnastics, but tonight it had been repurposed as a place for adults to take drugs. As I looked up, the rod holding the curtain started to shake, and I felt an anxious sensation in the back of my chest, as if someone had released a beast into the night. Someone hugged me from behind and their sweat left my back cool to the touch.

How are you doing, when did you get here, my friend the Fox asked. He smelled like soil.

In the bathroom stall, the Fox cut a few lines on the backseat of the toilet. An engraving on the back of the stall read "U R GAY." A laugh formed in the back of my throat, and the Fox turned solemn suddenly, miming a salute: Thank you, thank you, I had forgotten, he said to the door. When laughter trickled in from the stall next door, I held the bag up to him, but he shook his head and pointed to his tongue. He had had some earlier.

On the dancefloor, I felt as if my body and the world were built of the same clay. I understood that my feet were below my head. That my arms were beside my torso and that I had five toes at the ends of two legs. In the fog, these extensions of myself felt emphati-cally, angrily, in their right place, as if they wanted to be elsewhere.

I pleated myself into the music, into the corners of the bass. Every offbeat had a loose hi-hat to it, a shimmery, airy, hissing sound that made the heaviness of the bass feel like the release of a thousand hydraulic pistons. It was easy to forget that the music was sound and not actually something solid, because I felt like I was swimming in something unctuous and stupid, a clear molasses that covered my throat and singed my eyes, a geyser flowing in and out of me, until there were no fires left to extinguish.

The Rabbit, Part 2

Later that night, at the warehouse down the road from the General's Market, the music was loud and rude. I put my jacket down and walked over to my friend to survey the room, if there might be someone to talk to. The music here was soft and springy. The lyrics from the pop music encouraged conversation in a way that techno foreclosed, and I appreciated this feeling of openness and possibility, letting the excited chatter soak into me. I found my friend, but he was occupied, his arm around someone's waist, his fingers looped around their belt buckle.

I took a walk to let off some steam, strayed away from the warehouse and found myself walking toward the shore, which was visible from the club's front door. I dipped my feet in. It was cool and slippery.

In a flash of certainty, like a stone falling into a well, I removed my clothes. The banks of the lake were sloped and rocky, stinging the bottom of my feet. The light from the city cast a grey net onto the underside of the clouds.

I slipped into the water and swam towards the other bank, wading past lily pads that looked more like cacti up close. I drummed my fingers on their flat, round heads. Under the water, the electric light made the water look like a memory. I had lost the shore beneath me, and suddenly I was scared, thinking about what my mother had said all those years ago, even if I was sure that this was not the lake at the center of the city she had spoken about. I imagined being held up by the bones of lovers below and by the sky above, with its own nations of people in planes coming and going. The sound of a low, resounding bell, for alms, wafted over the water and I thought of home. I would leave tomorrow.

Music Heals: Lydo

Harry Burke

1.

When I dance, I love to respond to changes in the bassline, dipping a shoulder or raising a finger as a DJ breaks new rhythmic ground. In Lydo's sets, transitions often catch me out. A beat will slide into the mix some steps before or after the obvious drop, and a darting, celestial melody will glide in a few-and-a-half bars later.

Elegant and elusive, Lydo's sound departs from those established in cities like Detroit and Berlin, techno's meccas. This was underscored at Knockdown Center in March, when the Brooklyn-based DJ opened for Ben Klock and Robert Hood. A Berlin native and Berghain resident since 2005, Klock's sound is spare and heavy. Propelled by thick kicks and warm hi-hats, his tracks feature catchy flourishes and thunderous drops. A founder of Detroit's legendary Underground Resistance, Hood's techno is minimal and melodic, distinguished by its soulful groove and solid, four-on-the-floor rhythm.

Lydo's signature, by contrast, is their teasing syncopation. In their sets, hooks and basslines are frequently suspended or deferred.

Different ideas are often explored in a mix's upper and lower ranges, producing a doubling that is by turns queer, trans, and diasporic. Queer because it embraces the "ecstatic temporality," in the words of queer theorist José Esteban Muñoz, of being in multiple places simultaneously. Trans in that it moves between positions and finds meaning in this movement. Diasporic in the sense that it embraces the improvisational, in-between space in which, as postcolonial scholar Homi Bhabha notes, "the meaning and symbols of culture have no primordial unity or fixity." In its joyful multiplicity, Lydo's sound speaks to many forms of difference.

Lydo's parents met as refugees leaving Vietnam in the 1980s. The DJ was born in the Philippines, where they lived for twelve years, before moving to California—they speak with hints of a Filipino accent. Their music can be thought of as a soundscape of the Vietnamese diaspora, one historically shaped by its rejection of French colonialism and US imperialism. From the work of artists such as Trinh T. Minh-ha, Dinh Q. Lê, and An-My Lê, to authors like Viet Thanh Nguyen and Monique Truong, there is an expressive tradition that has carved out a space between the discourses of each invasive power, refusing assimilation into either. This tendency is exemplified by, for instance, Dinh's photo-weavings, which interlace documentary images with Hollywood film stills about the Vietnam war and draw upon traditional grass-mat weaving techniques. Lydo's sets, which slip between techno's dominant European and North American vernaculars, propel this lineage in the sonic realm.

2.

In 2017, Lydo began selling bags and other club apparel via X-TRA. SERVICES, a ravewear brand that soon evolved into a series of underground raves. The party is now hosted at Basement in Maspeth, Queens, where Lydo is a resident DJ. At the beginning of this year, X-TRA.SERVICES printed an ad in *Hii Magazine* that stated, in bold, italicized script, music heals, underlining the ethic that drives the platform.

This month, X-TRA.SERVICES released Lydo's first EP, *Hand of God* (2023), a collaboration with fellow Brooklyn-based producer Tomás Urquieta. "Pioneer Spirit," the throbbing, atmospheric opener, shows off the duo's inventive sound design, where metallic twitches pair with oozing, liquidlike bass. Aquatic pings provide a sense of depth, while tension builds through a suspended mid-layer that fades before the chord progression resolves. The title track blends quickfire percussion with a catchy synth line that quits the mix tantalizingly soon. It hovers in the mid-to-high range, with bouncing kicks, but no discernible bassline, its body provided instead by a sequence of mechanical growls. "Overture" is a pulsating techno tango, perfect for cutting up the dancefloor. "Coil," the record's closing statement, takes us deeper into the club. A tense, knifelike rhythm drives the song forward, while snares and a series of machinic flourishes are scattered between beats. Discordant textures thread together in a manner that entices and haunts.

In April, Lydo and Urquieta both played *X-TRA.SERVICES* at Basement. While Knockdown Center is a large, open hall, with rows of bass bins to compensate for the large windows that flank the dancefloor, Basement, located below a former door factory, is a more compact space, where bass reverberates off the curved brick walls. Its main floor plays techno, while a second space, Studio, leans toward house. Unlike Knockdown Center, Basement has a door policy. The lighting, a medley of red beams and flashing white floodlights, contrasts with most partygoers' black attire. *X-TRA.SERVICES* nights draw crowds for the music, rather than the vibes – the vibes, as a result, are welcoming.

I caught up with Lydo after their set, and they showed me a draft of the *Hand of God* artwork on their phone. Its central motif is an enigmatic, abstract symbol that is set to repeat on each of the label's upcoming releases. A layer of thin, red scratches evokes the industrial sounds that are woven through the record. In the background, two faint palimpsests of the EP's title suggest an infinite regress.

3.

During busy periods, I like to go out sober. I'll wake early and arrive for the last, dazzling stretch of a party. Afterward, I often meet friends for food, or wander to a museum—even sober, I need to come down.

I was drifting through the Met one afternoon, bass echoing in my ears, when I passed Kandinsky's *Improvisation 27 (Garden of Love II)*, made in 1912. Kandinsky referred to his paintings as impressions, improvisations, or compositions—his improvisations are expressions of interiority, or "inner nature." *Improvisation 27* features three imprecise sketches of a couple embracing. The figures are surrounded by a medley of vibrant, watery colors, punctuated by snaking black squiggles and murky, dark paint. An encounter with Austrian-American composer Arnold Schoenberg's atonal music in the early 1910s drove Kandinsky to distill painting to what he saw as its essential elements: color and form. When viewed sequentially, his paintings from this period are exhilarating, as they edge closer and closer to what was then known as "non-objective" art. *Improvisation 27* teeters on the edge of full abstraction.

Kandinsky was strongly influenced by mysticism as well as music. As it was for other modernists like Swedish painter Hilma af Klint, abstraction was a means to convey the inner life of things. Kandinsky sought to challenge the "nightmare" of materialism that, as he argues in his polemic *Concerning the Spiritual in Art* (1911), defined the culture of his day. His esotericism was inspired by theosophists like Helena Blavatsky and Rudolf Steiner, as well as the eschatology— the theology of death, judgment, and the soul's final destination—of Eastern Orthodoxy.

Kandinsky believed that art, like music, makes the soul vibrate. It's easy to dismiss this idea as unscientific, but recent developments in neurology corroborate this intuition. In his work on polyvagal theory, neuroscientist Stephen Porges demonstrates how social interactions affect the autonomic nervous system. The vagus nerve—the long, wandering nerve that connects the brain to the gut, and controls our autonomic nervous system—responds to our environment. Certain audio frequencies can have a soothing effect on this nerve and produce a feeling of safety—YouTube hosts a cottage industry of "miracle tones."

The artist's breakthrough came in 1913, when he produced *Composition VII*. The large, raucous composition is considered the artist's first, wholly abstract work. Its busy center is a tangle of black scribbles and scars. Uncategorizable forms and watery hues of red, yellow, green and blue repeat throughout the canvas. Colors darken toward the upper and right edges of the composition. Art historians narrate the painting as a reflection on the Biblical themes of resurrection, Judgment Day, the flood, and the Garden of Eden.

Kandinsky's work chimes with the aniconic nature of raving. Even where raves allow photos, it's rare to see someone document the dancefloor. It's implicitly understood that cameras compromise safety, and that there's a richer atmosphere when partygoers are attuned to their environment. In its fugitive relationship to documentation, techno aligns with the nonrepresentational dimension of the modernist artist's oeuvre. It might just be the afterglow of the dancefloor, but there's something about *Composition VII* that, to me, invokes the blurry chaos of a rave better than the press portraits, architectural photos, graphic flyers, and other stock imagery in techno's visual ecosystem.

As critics like Clement Greenberg contend, high modernism is defined by its preoccupation with the material conditions of representation. This mindset is epitomized in Kandinsky's reduction of painting to its primary attributes. The rave reanimates a painting like *Composition VII*, as I see it, because it replicates its logic of abstraction, not in the reified arena of the canvas, but in the ecstatic, contingent reality of social space. The rave, if we follow Kandinsky, is a spiritual experience. Although it's not only the soul that vibrates, but the collective body.

The arc of the modern master's career operates like a commercial techno track. His sequence of paintings up to 1913 builds a tension that grows until *Composition VII*, the alleged invention of abstraction, and the mother of all drops. Lydo's work breaks from this paradigm—their anti-epiphanic music is defined by deft layering and minor transitions. It enacts the type of disidentification from the mainstream that, as Muñoz proposes, is the offbeat heart of queer worldmaking.

In September, I woke early again to catch Lydo close the penultimate night of *Atonal*, a storied sonic and visual art festival held at Berlin's Kraftwerk, a vast former power plant near the Spree. They played for over four hours in Tresor, in the building's cellar. The first half was bold, brooding techno, escorting ravers into midmorning. Midway, the artist cut the sound momentarily, before exploding into a shiny, house-y groove. I live for the last hours of

a night, when most people have left and the dancefloor trans-
forms into a site of unfiltered expression. Tresor's interior is dim
and brutalist— DJs play behind a metal grille. The last section of
Lydo's set was vivid and brilliant; it was as if they were painting
the dancefloor in melting, moving colors. I left the club at noon in
shimmering sunlight.

Seedlings
Zoë Beery

1.

In the early months of 2018, my friend J. and I developed a ritual. One Saturday a month, he'd show up on my stoop at 2 a.m., both of us bleary off our disco naps. We'd get in a car and go to a low-slung building in Bushwick whose facade looked like the outside of a saloon in a Western movie. Inside was a disused banquet hall fashioned into a simulacrum of Berlin. Black clothes, hard techno, lots of drugs. Neither of us had been to Berlin, but we understood it as a place where the rules were not quite so constricting, and the music was really good.

The ritual continued like so: buy a mate, take MDMA, and talk about anarchism. One night, we stood on a balcony overlooking the dance floor, watching the separate movements of three hundred strangers cohere around Mary Yuzovskaya's hypnotic pounding. It was autonomy in motion, a collective experience created by individual choice in consideration of the whole. J. turned to me, his pupils crowding out the whites of his eyes, and yelled, "This is it! This is the revolution!" It was the kind of proclamation that only happens when you're rolling, something that feels so pure and urgent that you have to shout it even though it's ridiculous. At that moment, the lights flashed to red, then off to black, the colors of the anarchist flag, and we didn't stop laughing for five minutes.

I had been going to demos and actions since I was twelve. Raving had only come to me in the previous year, and I was convinced that it was revolutionary. How else to explain my friendship with J.? It started the year before at *Sustain-Release*, when he wandered up to me and my friend S. at the fire pit at 3 a.m. on Sunday morning looking for someone to talk to about autonomous organizing. How else to explain that we kept making more friends at demos who turned out to be ravers, and friends at raves who turned out to be leftists? I read about field raves in Britain in the early 1990s that in retrospect have been interpreted as revolts against Thatcherite austerity. I read about how Berghain started as an anarchist squat amidst the rubble of the Berlin Wall. I went to raves that fundraised against ICE. I started a zine with S. about the rave as liberation.

At the demos we all went to, we heard the classic chant: "We are unstoppable! Another world is possible!" The one without prisons, borders, violent hierarchies. Possible, sure, but impossibly far away. Then we went to the rave together, and when it was a good night, we stepped into the other world. It usually appeared around 3 a.m., when the amateurs left, and ended whenever sunlight first pierced our field of vision. I call it the time between yesterday and tomorrow. McKenzie Wark calls this "the time where there is more time." Henri Lefebvre, who I don't think ever went to a rave but would probably have liked them, calls it "appropriated time," the time we take back from the rhythms of capitalism and use for our own purposes: "It is a time that forgets time, during which time no longer counts (and is no longer counted). It arrives or emerges when an activity… is in harmony with itself and with the world. It has several traits of self-creation or of a gift rather than of an obligation or an imposition come from without."[1] Because rave time is appropriated from capitalism, we can abandon the strictures that bind us and try out something else. The hammer of the beat cracks the grip of subjugation.

I found that moving with my friends in appropriated time strengthened our bonds in the streets. As we pulled up our bandanas and stared down the cops, we knew the vision we were fighting for, because we had been there over the weekend. Solidarity and techno felt the same in our bodies—explosive, totalizing, exhilarating. In my first few years of raving, I would look around at the crowd and assume it was made up of radicals I hadn't met yet, strangers who also heard liberation in the speakers. The anarchist and the raver both count police and real estate as enemies, and the need to destroy both seemed so intuitive to me that I could not imagine anyone at the party felt differently.

I simply hadn't met enough of the people I was dancing with. One night, I made a friend on the dancefloor, and found out the next day that she worked at Palantir, and so did another guy I saw around all the time. Someone I recognized from the latest hours at the best parties turned out to work at a government office whose mandate was to bring raving under the purview of the state. I ran into one of New York's headline DJs during the 2020 uprising, one who had soundtracked many of my hours of appropriated time, and she told me that she had never read the news until that month. She was thirty-seven. The people around me on the dancefloor were there to escape, like me, but they weren't doing much to change the conditions we were escaping from. There was nothing political about any of it. The last time I went to the party where J. and I had first seen revolution in the dancefloor, there were uniformed NYPD officers at the door. The promoters didn't want to get shut down, so they asked the cops for permission to throw a rave, and agreed to their every demand.

2.

In the winter of 2021, a friend from Montreal who showed up unannounced sometimes in New York at raves, other times at an autonomous organizing space in Ridgewood, posted a video of a renegade on some train tracks. It looked like the kind of thing we couldn't get away with in New York. I asked him where it was. "Atlanta," he told me. "Are you hooked into Stop Cop City?"

A year and a half earlier, on June 12, 2020 an Atlanta cop had shot and killed an unarmed Black man named Rayshard Brooks in the parking lot of a Wendy's. George Floyd had been murdered less than three weeks before, and the next day, Atlantans burned that Wendy's to the ground. In spring of 2021, the mayor of Atlanta announced her solution to police brutality: a $90 million training facility, to be built on land in the unincorporated outskirts of the city that was currently a forest and had previously been a prison farm. Its marquee innovation was a mock town where the cops could practice putting down mass urban revolt. Another 2020 uprising would not be tolerated. Organizers in Atlanta dubbed the plan Cop City.

By the time I saw my friend's video, a few dozen of these organizers had started a full-time encampment in the forest to physically stop Cop City from being built. The ravers in the movement, and there were many, insisted on throwing parties almost every month because their vision of a world without Cop City included having fun. Later, one of them told me that the forest was the only place left in Atlanta for raving, because the same police that would train at Cop City had collaborated with the real estate industry to shut down warehouse parties, in preparation for rezoning abandoned industrial parks into condos and upscale retail. As ravers, they understood the stakes of the movement: a future where raves and trees give us life, or one where police take both and kill us.

The encampment survived the winter, and then the spring. Environmentalists, schoolteachers, prison abolitionists, and artists joined the crust punks. From afar, it seemed to me that the forest defense was working because it operated like a good rave. A large group of people, many of them strangers, had converged to see what would happen when they tried to do something together, even if they had different reasons for doing it and no particular outcome was guaranteed.

In June, a call echoed across Signal group chats: come to Atlanta for a week of action in July, and see what it's like to live in the other world that's possible. Six of us bought flights. There was J., of course, and D., who we'd met in a yurt at Nowadays; our three-person group chat was named after Mark Fisher. I'd met N. because we simultaneously had the same idea during the 2020 uprising, to collect earplugs from shuttered nightclubs and distribute them to street medics to guard against NYPD sound cannons. Her oldest friend, G., had partied in Berlin and joined an occupation against a coal mine in rural Germany. Our friend L., who N. had met at a New Wave night in Chicago, was the only one who had been to Atlanta. These were the people I trusted with a trip across state lines to do the most militant thing I'd ever done, and I had met all of them through raving. (At the last minute, J. got too sick to come, which was devastating.)

The climate of summer in Atlanta reminded me of the unventilated back room of a chicken and pizza shop in Brooklyn that hosted raves before Covid. In both, oxygen was replaced by moisture. Otherwise, the forest was spectacular, light dappling through the pine trees, a creek running past our tents, salamanders in the underbrush, birds overhead. A sign nailed to a tree trunk marked the entrance to the encampment: *You are now leaving the U.S.A.* We entered unending appropriated time, which we filled with walks, workshops, cooking, reading, and conversations with strangers about the yearslong political journeys that brought us to the forest.

There was a rave on Saturday night to cap off the week of action. Glow sticks sketched a path on the forest floor toward a clearing sheltered by an enormous blue tarp, where five dozen people danced in all directions. Other than all the camo, no one looked like a raver. The speakers were blown out and blasting a UK garage edit of "I Ain't Got You" by Alicia Keys. As twilight fell, even more people showed up, teenagers and wooks and punks, punctuating the DJ sets with cries of "Stop Cop City!"

It was not like any other rave I'd been to. It was a rave in the original sense, a completely renegade, DIY, free party that didn't seek to create a specific experience, but conjure an entirely new space. I realized I had in fact never been to a real rave, only varyingly expensive parties. Those parties were just rooms full of strangers unless the conditions aligned perfectly: the music, the crowd, the lights, whatever drugs I was on, they all had to coalesce into transcendence. I needed the music in particular to hypnotize me away from the world outside. But in the forest, I did not need hypnosis. I looked around at my friends, these relationships that intertwined raving with a belief in the total transformation of the world. Here we were together, in the place we sought in Brooklyn at 5 a.m., but rarely found. And so it didn't really matter that the music was inconsistent, that the lights were bright, that people were twirling fiber-optic whips off to the side of the dancefloor. In the forest we had appropriated not just time, but the world itself. And in this place, the other world that's possible, there was still a rave, but one of celebration rather than escape.

3.

Raves are a threat to the order of things, and so the state must crush them to survive. But their threat is tiny, a night of rebellion that lasts for maybe ten hours. The repression is fairly small, too: a brief detainment, a fine, an impounded soundsystem. In the months after we visited the encampment, Stop Cop City grew into the most potent and entrenched threat the U.S. government had seen in years. A small group of anarchists and racial justice activists had become the focal point of global leftist organizing. The narrative was ironclad: why destroy a forest and replace it with cops?

Four months after the rave, once winter temperatures had shrunk the encampment, the police dragged six forest defenders out of their treehouses and charged them with domestic terrorism. Two months after that, the police shot a forest defender named Tortuguita fifty-two times during a raid near the forest dancefloor, and charged four more people there with domestic terrorism. In March, the police raided a music festival near the forest during another week of action and charged thirty-six people with domestic terrorism. There was supposed to be a rave that night, but it didn't happen.

The next month, as I cried with D. about all of it, they told me something they'd learned during a conversation in Atlanta. The founder of the Ridgewood organizing space, where our forest crew was spending increasing amounts of time, had been learning how to DJ before he was killed in a collision on the drive back from Standing Rock. He had apparently become convinced that transformational change would be possible only if it included raves.

J. had not been wrong on the balcony. It was not a coincidence that we had met at a for-the-heads techno festival, or that rave friends had led me to Atlanta, or that the forest encampment was founded partially by ravers, or that raves happened there all the time. We rave because it allows us to feel in our bodies a defiance of the lie that the world the cops impose on us is the only option. Raving is not a political act, or a utopia. But it contains the seed of revolution, if you give it some free water.

A Politics for the End of The World

Kumi James aka BAE BAE

I resent the forces of history that have violated communities and ecologies on this Earth. The embodied traumas of my ancestors pass through me, creating ruptures in time and the coherence of my being. As a thinker, artist, and space convener, I am compelled to *do* something about the current state of the zombified world, however limited. The events that I co-produce are not utopias, but rather experimental cultural practices combining dance, diverse bodies, music, illegal space, and relationality—all operating underneath the guise of a party.

How might we enact cultural practices that could uproot the dying world and propagate something new? This is something I am seeking to understand in the peripatetic timelines of underground spaces. I throw a rave in virtually abandoned warehouses in LA called *Hood Rave*. These are nights of play for queer and black desires. Sexual, friendly, flirtatious, aggressive, playful, and even combative expressions can all breathe in improvised ways. Transgressions, as much as we try to prevent them with our signage ("this is a consent-centered space," "no transphobia or homophobia") are inevitable, considering we cannot be rid of the socialization of the normative world. The goal is in part to create a space where violence can be dealt with in a comparatively safer way than in above-ground institutional space, through practices like transformative justice. We also attempt to center Black, Brown, queer, and trans people and their experiences.

Due to rising awareness of the profitability of underground events, raves in LA are expensive, so I have to use my marketing skills and play on some level of folks' desires for a unique nightlife experience. I'm not immune to strategically advertising the event in a way fitting of the capitalist system we inhabit—I create a space that is rarefied and desirable. There's a duplicity here. I know what appears attractive in online queer black Gen Z culture, from the newest song edits of hits by St. Louis female rapper Sexyy Red to twerk videos of girls and gays shaking ass. We sell the shadow to support the substance. There are potentially subversive representations held within this media, producing an energy that cannot be contained by the event or its promo. On a libidinal level, black and queer unfiltered relationality challenges what it means to be in a society of capitalistic control. The rave space itself is about letting the signification do its thing without attaching language to it. We call *Hood Rave* "a place where we can be free." We intentionally avoid spelling out exactly what that means.

Many brands have chosen to collaborate with emerging underground event producers, because they want to harness the energy that the black rave produces. Brands extract cultural capital for their inclusion of "alternative" black and brown bodies. After years of COVID-19 lockdowns and distancing measures, underground raves proliferated as pent-up social energy had to be expressed. After so much alienation, people thirsted for risky, sweaty proximity. A nostalgic craving emerged for the raves of the '90s and aughts, and the fantasy that your dream community could exist in a space held together by rhythm. As folks become alienated by a society that wants us all to be separated, ingesting social media alone, many people crave something else: the end of the world as we know it.[1] As rave and house music culture has been mainstreamed and platformed, many in the underground community have worked to raise consciousness about the black roots of techno and the continued presence of black electronic musicians.

Homo ≠ Homogenous

At *Hood Rave,* no one is turned away for lack of funds. Often white and monied folks contribute donations to support the coming together of our rave community, which is of marginalized folks. This kind of cross-racial and cross-class solidarity is an important part of overturning the world. It's a way folks can practice allyship and contribute to the third space[2] of the underground. It is also a kind of care that challenges the notion of siloed identities.

At a rave I threw earlier this year, I had booked Sheefy McFly, one of the current ghetto tech DJ/producers of Detroit, who is carrying on a tradition of black techno sonic technology. After providing a soundscape that successfully made most of the crowd ass-shake for over an hour, he went outside to smoke. A group of folks hanging outside started confronting everyone asking if there were any "cishet" people in the space. He told me that it was his signal to get the fuck out of there.

I don't know what the group intended to do with the cishets they did find in the space, but I find the moment to be indicative of some underlying issues with what it means to build community with black and queer people in LA. My goal with the booking was to bring a Detroit native who had roots in black techno, ghetto tech, and other raunchy black sonics. I had no interest in admonishing the partygoers, who were probably going to playfully ki about his "cishetness," but it raises some questions for me as a convener of people in space.

Mainly I'm wondering, at the end of the world: How can we attend to wide range of internal differences within black and queer community? How do we keep culture alive and complex and avoid creating a kind of insular cult?

Does identity politics sometimes reach its limit?

There's nothing homogenous about nightlife culture. In my own dealings in making a rave happen, I'm working with black, white, brown, mixed, straight, queer, trans, and gender nonconforming people in many different capacities. The club, techno, and house music we listen to that is loved by black queer people, was produced and engineered by a mix of folks of many ethnic, racial, and gender identities. Ultimately blackness is not a monolith, and neither is queerness. Is it possible to invent an ecosystem that is capacious enough to create space for our differences?

Many of us come together in the underground because we have felt cast out of "normative" society; we do not fit into traditional cisgendered, heterosexual, white, straight, monied, dimensions of the "human." It's empowering to experiment with the ways that we embody identity. Creating language for folks outside of the margins to construct their experience is essential for surviving this hellhole world. I wonder how we can better attend to the inherent inconsistencies and differences within our so-called "community." Can our cultural production be capacious enough to hold difference without hierarchizing and overly codifying it? Is there a pathway to creating the *new* through hybridized forms and identities without erasing history and while minimizing violence?

Hood Rave is made up of dykes, lesbians, fags, fag hags, mascs, femmes, nonbinary folks, trans folk, and, dare I say it. . . cishets? Though I emphasize that the space was built to center black queerness, it's not easy to pin down what that means. The English language has serious limitations when it comes to identifying things. Once you name something "black" and "queer" English seems to lock it up into an overdetermined category. But black queerness is complex, gummy, and mysterious.

I once heard Saidiya Hartman say that blackness has always been queer. Looking through the lens of Hortense Spillers's essay "Mama's Baby, Papa's Maybe," one might come to the same conclusion.[3] Spillers describes how African folks' flesh was coded into the white gender binary when they crossed the Atlantic and were named "black." Gender was a standard of measure of their economic value for the prospective slave master, as "male" and "female" slaves were attributed different sale prices. But did black people ever properly fit into the categories of "maleness" or "femaleness"? Sojourner Truth's provocative line of questioning "[A]nd ain't I a woman?" also comes to mind.

"I don't identify as a femme. I identify as a bulldagger," my professor Tiffany Willoughby-Herard once told me. Never before had I thought to use the word "bulldagger" to describe someone I cared about. It felt outdated and borderline offensive. The term I used for myself, "black femme," seemed gentler. However, this was a generational identity marker for Willoughby-Herard, my queer black mentor. Inhabiting the identity of a bulldagger was something she took pride in and inevitably had had to wrestle with over her lifetime. In this way identity is a slippery thing. Once you think you have a grasp of a collective group of people, the reality of who they are slips through.

Culture as Ecosystem

I am finding that the best model for thinking about difference and how it can help us build coalitional underground music community is looking at nature and how it grows and reproduces itself. Nature thrives most when it's a heterogeneous mix of varying life forms. An ecosystem of a coral reef might include fish, octopus, crabs, plankton, seaweed, coral, rock, and other entities. Predators and prey coexist even while inhabiting their antagonism. Together the ecosystems are held together by the tensions of difference and oppositions.

We might consider by contrast the western dominant agricultural system which often organizes itself via monocultures, the propagation of one kind of crop on a mass scale. With large-scale monocultural methods of farming, more of one crop can be produced, leading to larger profits, but the quality of a particular crop dwindles significantly over time. The lack of biodiversity creates more susceptibility to disease and a higher need for pesticides.

Extending this metaphor, sometimes I see in my community a lack of capacity to hold difference. This may be a natural consequence of the heteronormative violence and racial capitalism that seeks to enforce a homogeneity of the so-called "human," and a hierarchization that leads to the alienation of people at the margins of so-called normativity. Why would one not react in ways that excludes one's violator? There is also something scary about having to contend with another's human complexity if they do not fit easily into an identity-category. The question of who is in and who is out, like the ire towards "cishets" is often under the surface. Having a culture that is marginal becomes something people protect, for good reason. But the question is: when do the terms for coming together become too strict, cultish, or re-alienating?

What I propose through the practice of event production is that we create a culture with the capacity for expansiveness, to invent new ways of being, and that respect the opacity that we each contain. Nightlife, under the influence of the moon, lends itself to a kind of mystery, exploration, and experimentation of the self. Perhaps someone you see who is a "cishet" is in flux, on their own path of exploring their queerness. Maybe the light-skinned black girl you see dancing in the corner and think is privileged is actually houseless. Maybe the hard lines around whether someone is "in" or "out" of the black queer club is a reproduction of the same binaristic lines that normalcy encourages. Instead, we could be like wildlife, constantly emerging and mutating as something else, even if that is for the ephemeral time of the underground.

We have seen many periods where cultures meet and create new hybrid forms. Techno itself is a hybridized form of black sound infiltrating analog and digital technologies meant for traditional purposes. Black people fucked that shit up! New music and language have emerged from the contact between black sonic forces and classical western instruments and language. Think jazz and Jamaican patois, the foundational explorations in black music and sound system culture. England is a particularly useful example when you think of reggae influencing ska and rock. Unique class and ethnic solidarities emerged in London in the state-subsidized council houses, where black folks were connecting with other ethnic minorities and poor and working class white people to create innovative sounds like dubstep, grime, and garage. These hybrids were born out of proximity and the intersections of communities.

I'm not promoting some kind of easy raceless or genderless politics, that ignores colonial history and ongoing violence. I would never promote a Western style of "diversity and inclusion," which is really code for the managing of desires of the racial/gendered/sexual other, often conducted to help integrate people into a system where they compete to "represent" the interests of their identity groups. I'm more interested in us looking at how we can challenge and create beyond the McDonalds-style globality and its neoliberal politics of representation. We may have never consented to be here, but now that we're here, how can we *un*make this world? We may live in late capitalism, but if it's a zombie—it will never die unless we reframe our collective imaginations.

Mumbo Jumbo

My favorite example of thinking of a radical culture that could bring about the end of the world as we know it is Ishmael Reed's apocalyptic novel *Mumbo Jumbo*.[4] It hops and thrusts, leaps and twists backwards and forwards in time, much like the black plague that the book chronicles. In the book, the hegemonic white capitalist Atonist world is interrupted by the spread of *jes grew*, what Reed calls an "anti-plague." This anti-plague arrives in the form of people dancing, gyrating, speaking in slick jive talk, and being fully in a sense of their aliveness. It is a counterpoint to the Atonist path, that of the Wallflower Order, the dominant culture of existing not in the body but in some disassociated mind that seeks to control and order life to the point of destroying it. Mumbo Jumbo is an uncontrollable force that goes against the world as we know it. It is an embodied culture that is constantly on the move, incapable of being apprehended, ever changing, and borderless. It privileges expansion, connection, creation, and fecundity. It respects death, but not as some final ending. As depicted in the Bakongo cosmogram, a pre-European Central African diagram of the circularity of life and death, there is always life after death, and death after life.

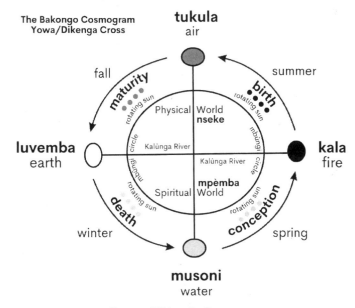

Source: Wikimedia Commons

Perhaps blackness and queerness aren't identities, but forces, like the anti-plague of *jes grew*. The force of the body and spirit finding a dimension of freedom immanent to every moment. They could be like a black hole, pulling us towards it so that we may enter new indeterminate spatial realities. Culture as compelling and infectious as *jes grew*. The blackness I'm considering has other names outside of the English language. Perhaps ultimately race is only a starting point for the exploration of something beyond the notion of humanity: something more and something less than the so-called "human." I'm interested in convening spaces that allow us to access and come into our identities in ways that avoids stagnation. What I would give to attend a Warehouse party in Chicago in the '90s! People of all kinds, driven by the promise of pulsating rhythm to liberate them from their daily identitarian trappings, if only for those moments on the dancefloor (in the dark, maybe off a bump of cocaine). In this way the warehouse party can become an experimental space for the complexification of human life.

I'm not saying we do away with identity completely. Of course it's important to speak up for oneself and one's being in a world that seeks your destruction. I see this very acutely with my trans siblings in my community. My provocation is for us to seek more creative ways of forming and sustaining community than merely flipping the existing dominant racial and gender hierarchy upside down, placing straight white folks at the bottom. Though that may feed our egos, there are more creative possibilities in the practice of *un*making the world.

Perhaps attending to our differences at the margins is the only way to avoid recreating the homogenous nature of a dominant culture that seeks to destroy what is "other." Third spaces like the underground rave alchemize their differences from dominant culture to generate portals for something *other* to emerge. Inventively allowing space for the complexities, contradictions, and blurred nature of identity can be another energetic source for non-hegemonic cultural production. The goal for my underground event space project is to make revolution irresistible to us all, which simultaneously means making collectivity irresistible.[5] We will never bring back the possibility of a future in our silos. We must remain open to our enigmas and the generativity of touching the void.

Mexican Nights
Geoffrey Mak

We had come to Mexico City for New Year's in a bid to save our relationship. I was feeling ungrateful, depressed. After a year of abundance, good luck, and careerist accomplishment that spiked bitterness upon my enemies, I had fallen into a vicious fit of anhedonia because, it turns out, wanting something you don't have makes you feel more alive than actually having it. When I texted this to D, he wrote, "Go do some jumping jacks." So when I told him that his neglect to show his own boyfriend basic care had triggered thoughts of breaking up, he had a bouquet of roses and lilies sent to my Brooklyn apartment and we had passionate sex and for a while our problems went away. We had been together nine months. What had begun with an eagerness so bewildering it got me to say, unironically, "Meeting you makes me believe in God," had since gear-shifted into—for him—a reasonable mix of tolerance and lust, and—for me—the tradeoff of normalizing orgasm-optional sex in exchange for having a sensible social teammate.

"I'll pay for the hotel," D decided, and I felt like a princess.

Our first night in the city, we went to a dinner party in Condesa hosted by a muscle queen with distracted eyes and a cropped sweater that showed the strip of skin across his V-lines. He looked like a himbo. Except I had just read his Wikipedia on the car ride over, which said he was the AIDS activist and investigative journalist who broke the story that the Sacklers were pushing Oxy throughout the opioid epidemic. His two-bedroom apartment, in a building whose doorman photographed each of our passports before letting us up the elevator, had a balcony, not "furniture" but "pieces," and a wall made almost entirely out of glass.

"Can I tell him how much you pay for this apartment?" my friend asked the journalist, standing in his office. On the lacquered credenza was a family-size bottle of fish oil.

He looked at me. "I pay $1000."

We probably shouldn't have been there. We weren't bad people. We were a despised class of self-despising freelancers: artists who got into MacDowell but had no gallery representation, or the kind of writers who would never get into MacDowell but wrote "copy," or subsisted, as one dinner guest put it, "entirely on the favors of others." He was an American from Colorado, living off the money an advertising consultant based in Berlin paid him to read an entire year of the *Angelicism* Substack and report back his findings. Many of us were on Medicaid. We could not honestly tell you how a mortgage worked. We each knew precisely one celebrity, but probably not two.

At dinner, it was someone I'll call Chloe, like Chloe Sevigny if she were trans. She sat along the couch under pink-tinted lights, legs elegantly arranged like sliding book spines on a shelf. Her hair, stark as redwood, and her black dress gave her body the character of a cello. If you made eye contact, she knew how to lower her gaze and smile.

The situation was a marginalized people searching for a mainstream aspirational icon, and the story was Chloe. Socialite of the demimonde, she had risen from DIY nightlife and climbed her way to the Hollywood big screen. She was easy to root for. Assumed in her biography, regardless if it's true, is an empowerment narrative of being forced to question at a young age, like a baby on acid, every premise of reality and safety, down to the facts of one's flesh and bones, called to remake oneself in the image of inclusivity and self-determination at a moment when, excuse me, universal access to transition care is the single, most urgent civil rights fight of our era. She made being queer look dignified. Like Jesus, she had suffered, suffered so that her struggle could pinkwash the exploitation and sexual excess of a globalized queer generation made complacent after marriage equality, out here doing the gentrification tour between New York and Berlin and now Mexico City. As we were microwaving our brain cells, Chloe's face was beamed across the world to kindergarteners in Cincinnati, or ravers slinging Telfar bags watching American TV with Turkish subtitles.

After dinner, we all split up into cars headed to *Brutal MX*, a weekly queer party in Centro. At coat check, I could only admire the pragmatism of the fat, bored attendant shoving my mohair sweater and blue Balenciaga parka into a yellow plastic bag. We found Chloe by finding not her, but the group of friends huddling around her, as if protecting a Fabergé egg slowly rotating in space. Her voice projected at a touch slower when everyone else spoke a touch faster. Every line was treated like the wit of scripted dialogue.

"You've never been to Burning Man?" I asked.

"I'm only going if someone's flying me out on a private jet," she said.

"It's the third pillar of rave culture: Berghain, Ibiza, and Burning Man."

"The three genders," she said.

D and I decided to snort ketamine in separate trips to dodge security. I walked past the woman guarding the door to the bathroom, and accidentally caught her eyes. I knew she wanted me to know that she knew. Without D, I stole the chance to snort two bumps instead of one. It had been months since I last snorted K. I no longer buy or carry ketamine with me in New York, and I could not remember the last time I had it. I also could not remember the last time I had ejaculated.

Back from the bathroom, the edges of my vision began to blur. The venue had sticky, black-and-white tiled floors and an elevated dancefloor made of plywood, which muddied the sound. On either side of the DJ booth were shirtless go-go dancers with vacant eyes. I never got the set times so I didn't know who was playing, but she knew how to speed up a room, when to slow it down, and when to serve the room the basic four-to-the-floor they came to hear. You either do or don't need this sound. It can come from portable speakers, a Funktion-One, or even a laptop, but when you really need this sound, it doesn't matter where you get it from. I thought of Warhol's *Marilyn* paintings, sequenced one after another in endless repetition; no matter how many times her face deteriorates, her essence remains. Like a kick drum. The icon of a kick is indistinguishable from the kick itself. Form is essence. The sound always arrives whole and sovereign, becoming for me, at this moment in time, the only reality. I and my desire were but an extension of that conception. Knowing that I could find this warm thump, this beat, in essentially any city I decided to fly into, swaddled me in a sinister comfort. *Even in Arcadia, there I am.*

*

"Sometimes when you're on K, you're so high I'm like, Why am I even here?" D said at the hotel.

We were getting ready for Jeppe Ugelvig's New Year's party, on the occasion of his thirtieth birthday. Packing for my flight, I had flung clothes all across my couch and bed. I thought I might wear head-to-toe Raf Simons to the party, in honor of the late menswear line that had taught me everything, until D had said, "With *those* boots?"

Jeppe is the editor of *Viscose*, a fashion journal that has published the best fashion criticism in the last ten years because it has zero fashion advertisers. Legend has it that when Martin Margiela exhibited his first foray into art at Zeno X Gallery in Antwerp, he was in talks with a European museum that was interested in acquiring his sculptures. But after the board read Jeppe's pan of Margiela's show in *Frieze,* they declined to buy a single piece.

For the weekend, Jeppe had rented out a villa with two pianos, a mezzanine, and an erect setup of aristocratic armor by the fireplace. Jeppe swiveled around to appear in each conversation circle for exactly seven minutes. The way he smiled close-lipped seemed to say "Well, hello" and "Who did you think I was?" and "We're in on this together."

On a caramel couch, I got locked into a conversation with a neurologist who was studying the long-term effects of ketamine, about which he could tell me basically nothing. He had a strange affect: skittish, impatient, as if eager for the conversation to end, which made me want to end it, except he kept talking. More than once, he said, "I'm so glad I met you," which overcompensated for what, exactly, I wasn't sure. We went upstairs to do a bump of coke, and about a half hour later, I felt distracted and impatient and was waiting for each conversation to end.

Everyone here was an editor of a magazine. *Document Journal, i-D, PIN–UP, BUTT.* I was about to say I felt out of place, except I forgot that I'm also an editor of a magazine. Up in Jeppe's bedroom, we all did lines of mystery coke on a generous silver platter, grinding our teeth til midnight. Sitting to Jeppe's right on the bed, D was offering around our remaining bag of ketamine as five or six magazine editors dipped their keys, and I knew D was doing this so we wouldn't have any left at the rave.

We were all going to *Por Detroit* later, a queer party that our friend who was DJing earlier that night had recommended we go to in the group chat. On the car ride there, D asked, "Who was that white guy you were talking to earlier?"

"Some neurologist," I said.

"He seemed into you."

"That's definitely not what was happening."

Or was it? When we arrived, we extended our arms as we were patted down. It was a good thing they didn't search our wallets because I hadn't bothered taking my ecstasy pills out of mine, something I never forgot to do when I lived in Berlin, which meant I was getting sloppy this time of night.

The party was at Ex Fabrica—"ex-factory" in Spanish—a flour plant from a century ago. It's an open-air building with two floors: the first had a massive dancefloor with light projections above the DJ booth, playing big-room techno. You had to wait in line to get to the upstairs floor—smaller, gayer, music not as good—which is where all our friends were, because New Yorkers just love hanging where you have to queue to get into. On the far side were large bean-bag benches, where I sat next to an acquaintance—some rumored millionaire—while he dosed milliliters of GBL and coke, reclining like a satyr. "He was like, 'Just because you're bored of Bushwick doesn't mean you get to colonize Mexico,' and I was like, 'Watch me.'" He waved an imaginary wand in the air.

I thought of *Maria Full of Grace*, when she has to swallow, one after another, packets of white powder to smuggle on the plane. "Bolivian Marching Powder," is what they called it in *Bright Lights Big City*. I thought of *Rotting in the Sun*, but my brain short-circuited. The ecstasy was hitting.

Back on the dancefloor, my eyes fixated on a Mexican raver boy who wasn't at the party earlier, but I could tell he knew everyone in our group of thirty or so. He had large ears, and thick sensual brows. I spent most of my life using my own ugliness as an excuse to feel sorry for myself, which led me to think I could gawk at the bold and beautiful as long as I wanted, convinced they don't see anyone except those who look like them. Fashion was a way to get people to look at me back, and the rave was an excuse to wear the most extravagant looks. But old habits die hard. I kept staring at the raver boy, until he caught my gaze, and I looked away. D, beside me, was dancing with his eyes closed. Where was the neurologist? Back in New York, I had brought up opening our relationship—wouldn't that be the gay thing to do?—though D had emphatically declined. Scanning the dancefloor, I caught eyes again with the raver boy, who I realized had been watching me, and as my eyes darted away, I thought, I could have this. *If I* wanted. I looked back at D, whose eyes were open now, and I had the sudden urge to pull him closer. Perhaps for the first time, he looked distinctly *cute* to me, if not because I discovered I had the ability to hurt him.

Suddenly, there was a commotion. Something had caught D's attention, and I glanced to see what it was, what everyone was looking at. Across the crowd, I saw the tops of everyone's heads, at different heights, swerving up and down, like a wave agitated by a great storm—but there was a parting in that wave. Ravers were gyrating to the beat, but as if in slow motion, a group was proceeding elegiacally across the wooden floor, very slowly. There were three or four of them, heads bowed in intense concentration. Carried on their shoulders was Chloe. Her body lay limp, arms around the others' backs, head leaned back to show the curved line of her pale neck looking bluish in this light. Her eyes were closed or half-lidded, and as her friends cleared the path before her, her head lolled down. People cupped each other's ears, whispering. D is usually good about being discreet, except he was blatantly staring now, so I was, too. Chloe's friends carried her down to the side, across one of the bean bags, and then gathered around her, closing in to the point where I could no longer see her body.

Considering how addicted I used to be to ketamine, I have only been carried off the dancefloor once in my life. It happened at Nowadays. Two big bumps of that New York shit, and I had slipped into a K-hole, a galactic dimension so far out I could not command my muscles, and I did not even feel the arms of my friends carrying me; I felt like I was floating, until I woke up on the couch upstairs where someone in clown makeup was trying to get me to drink some pineapple juice. Did you even know Nowadays has an upstairs?

This was during a phase when, twice a month, I could burn through a gram and a half by myself in my bedroom on a weeknight, and just eat the $150 I sometimes got paid for writing an entire piece. After I started dating D, my ketamine cravings evaporated—that unannounced 8 p.m. itch to obliterate myself to the same Soundcloud mixes I played forty, sixty times for this exact purpose. I was no longer visited by that aching, humiliating loneliness I had felt, but for years convinced myself was "solitude," and therefore good for me.

I looked at D now, his hair clamped on his scalp as his hair product dripped down his sideburns from sweat. I had always had a superiority complex that we hadn't met on an app. We were at the private afterparty for a mutual friend's film screening at the Roxy in New York, and we locked eyes across the room. Before we were even dating, he moved upstate for a one-month writer's residency. He didn't ask, "Are you coming to visit me," but "When?" We had the entire house to ourselves: a small cottage, beside a renovated chapel that had been broken up into a workshop and art gallery. Lying on my back, having just woken up from an afternoon nap, he climbed onto me, fully clothed, and kissed my face over and over again, like a guppy, and I could not stop smiling because I knew that at last, my loneliness was ending.

On our sixth-month anniversary, we decided to get dinner at El Quijote at the Chelsea Hotel. "Should we get a room?" he asked, winkingly. Instead, we went to his apartment in Chinatown, and we clumsily fumbled out of our clothes, our teeth still tasting of garlic. We fucked for an hour. "Hold on, can we take a break?" I said, my body suddenly shaking uncontrollably. I couldn't tell why. It's not like we were trying anything new. "Sorry, I think we need to stop," I said. Naked, I scurried to the bathroom, heart racing, skittish as my feet pressed on the cold tile, mortified that I had ruined this night. The next afternoon, the birds who usually sat on the electric wire were gone. D was peeling clementines when, apropos of nothing, he blurted, "Did I do something wrong last night?" I looked up from my laptop and saw his face, crestfallen, bruised by the tape reel of last night that had been looping in his mind ever since. He looked devastated that he could have done something to hurt me. Except all I could think of at the moment was, *Do you still want me?*

D was dancing with his back turned to me, but then I grabbed his shoulders, turned him around, and made out with him, sloppily like a dog. He smiled, surprised. "Hi," he said. On his face was straightforward, uncomplicated joy. I was so, so happy. I wanted him then, his joy, his thick dick, his chirpy voice, his exasperating need to always be right, or his compulsion to mock everything as "corny," excepting the time he gasped in awe when I showed him the new Phoebe Philo collection for the first time. It was so fucking cute. Even the bickering, I wanted. All of it was all I ever wanted. Then I had an epiphany worthy of the ecstasy that had caused it. Even if at times I hated him, I loved the hate, but I did not hate the love. It was *all love*, all the way down.

I heard a voice I recognized. I turned around. It was Chloe, standing directly behind me on the dancefloor. "What should we do now?"

she asked the tall, statuesque filmmaker standing beside her. He shrugged: Literally anything. Anything we want. Everyone around me had this stupid grin on their face as the sun rose. People were starting to put on sunglasses, key-dipping on the dancefloor. How long was the party going until? We would keep dancing if we had to, rotting in the sun like a pack of wild dogs. It was 2024, and Chloe had risen. We were all going to be okay. She had resurrected, and all of our sins would be forgiven.

Adult Entertainment

madison moore

1.

Lately, I've been thinking about queer nightlife, raving, dancing and partying as adult entertainment, *playtime* for adults who refuse—in whatever small ways—to live a normative life under capitalism.

2.

Queer theorists have long written about the possibilities of life in, through and beyond heteronormative structures of linear time and productivity, of cooking up something new and bold and exciting in queer time (bcc *Jack*). Adult entertainment, with its premium on play, pleasure and feeling, offers another way to think about the work dancefloors can do.

3.

Thirty-two. That's the age I discovered nightlife as a way of being in the world. It's not that I was new to nightlife or going out—far from it—but instead that at the age of thirty-two (*no longer a twink, not yet a zaddy*) I discovered the specificity of embracing nightlife as the way I wanted to be in the world.

4.

Like most messy gay college students, I spent my twenties rolling in and out of gay bars and clubs on my way to figuring out *who* and *how* I wanted to be. I loved the spectacle of going out and Saturday night, but it was not quite a way of life, just something I did because that's what I thought you were supposed to do in your twenties. This was pre-Grindr, for those who remember the ancient years. How else were you going to meet somebody? This is also what many sociological studies of nightlife tell us: that nightlife is a training ground for young people to figure out who they want to be and how to build out their social worlds.

5.

I made a lot of mistakes in these spaces, and I didn't always have a great time in them if I'm honest, but even a bad night didn't keep me from going out again.

6.

Some things I looked forward to and could only see at night: The Zand Collective at Le Bain; full frontal boners at Secrets; the looks at *Misshapes*; the gay glamour of Mr. Black. At a certain point on my nightlife journey, though, I ended up with a string of boyfriends who weren't really into going out, who low-key made me feel guilty that sometimes I wanted to be out at night instead of at home with them, and that kept me from throwing myself into the scene the way I wanted to. I stayed home when I really wanted to be out because I didn't have the language to explain that my love of nightlife was about a love of nightlife as theater, as fun, as community. Didn't mean I loved them any less.

7.

So it wasn't until I moved to London on a research fellowship in my early thirties—a fellowship focused on Black diasporic nightlife and social dance forms no less—during a period I like to think of as "The London Sessions," that I understood nightlife as an unruly, even disobedient way of being in the world. This was much different to the way I approached nightlife in my twenties, which was something I loved but did just because I liked it, because it was the weekend. Now here I was, far away from home. What's the point of moving to a totally new place if you're not going to reinvent yourself?

8.

Moving to London was a hard reset followed by a software update. I made friends in nightlife and my housemates were bartenders, promoters and DJs. We threw house parties that I still think about till this day. I started parties and discovered how to roam from one party to the next, then to the afters, then dealing with the chaos of the night bus journey from Elephant and Castle or Hackney Wick or Canary Wharf or Brixton or Peckham back home to London Fields (this was all all before the Night Tube kicked in), staying out until 7 a.m., sometimes waking up that early to go to the party.

9.

Everybody talks about how *young* they were when they first started going out. So young you got a fake ID. So young you had to sneak out to sneak in. So young the bouncer scrawled an X on your underage hand. By the age of thirty-two, I should have been done going out, right?

10.

Rave media and cultural commentary often position nightlife as a youth culture (bcc *Angela/Dick/Sarah*), and in some ways that's true.[1] Young people *are* the overwhelming majority at the function, and even beyond that, subcultural practices, slang, musical genres, and fashion trends often start with young people at the club, only later spreading out to the rest of us. The whole system is set up to privilege whatever is new now next, and that often means older artists and performers get overlooked, feeding straight into the narrative that nightlife is a youth culture, a time and set of experiences in your life with an expiration date.

11.

The thing about positioning nightlife as primarily a youth culture, though, is that it suggests nightlife is something only aimless young people without jobs or responsibilities do. Go out in your twenties, grow out of it, then become an adult by pivoting to feed the capitalist machine of labor and productivity. Anybody with *real* responsibilities wouldn't dare spend their hard-earned coin or free time in a shitty warehouse in Hackney Wick. Party when you're young, because the minute you get older, the crushing, depressing, all-consuming reality of life under capitalism kicks in. The minute you get older, rent is due and the bills must be paid and actually now they are late and you're working forty to fifty hours a week and you're exhausted but the deadlines keep piling up and you go to bed early or have a partner or kids or both and being a responsible adult means putting your own fun last.

12.

One of my favorite things about going out, though, has always been seeing older people at the club. I'm talking about folks in their forties, fifties, sixties, seventies, the kind of folks who have been everywhere, seen everything, who hold court at the bar while they lovingly shade all the young children. I want a multigenerational dancefloor, a packed party with a minimum age of thirty. I want dancefloors with folks like my Aunt Mildred (seventies), who recently told me "I'm gonna pop it till I can't no more."

13.

Older ravers complicate the idea that raving is a phase, that club culture is merely a youth culture, further demonstrating nightlife as a queer way of life. You could say I've been thinking a lot about nightlife and age because while I'm not getting any younger, the crowds surely are. But as I look around at my own nightlife community, I realize this motley crew of club kids are parents, musicians, activists, doctors, lawyers, scientists, painters, graphic designers, theater producers, creative directors, writers, freelancers, artists, and directors of centers and organizations with a mountain of responsibilities, yet all of them embracing nightlife as a way of being in the world.

14.

In his influential essay "Friendship as a Way of Life," Michel Foucault notices how the thing that trips people up about homosexuality isn't gay sex but a homosexual life. To be "gay," for Foucault, is about developing "a way of life," which "can be shared among individuals of different age, status, and social activity. It can yield intense relations not resembling those that are institutionalized (bcc *Foucault*)." Even the phrase "a way of life" suggests living in excess of norms and structures that dictate how we move. "A way of life" can lead to the development of a range of cultures, subcultures and intergenerational relationships.[2]

15.

Nightlife as a way of life isn't always fun. The rave isn't always a great time because somebody or some*thing* always fucks up the vibe (bcc *Kemi*).[3] The cops show up. Unwanted advances. Too much to drink. Music is bad, too loud, not your taste. Fights break out. Too hot. So-in-so can't stand so-in-so who just walked in. Drama, drama, drama. The side effect of thinking about nightlife and rave culture as something you do but grow out of with age means missing the opportunity to see the rave, the dancefloor, and the party as a reminder, even a call to action, to *play*: "a stepping out of 'real' life into a temporary sphere of activity with a disposition all of its own. . . Play. . . lies outside the reasonableness of practical life; has nothing to do with necessity or utility, duty or truth. (bcc *Johan*)."[4]

16.

Adult entertainment is a way of life that privileges *playtime,* the promiscuousness of feeling, and reclaiming your time in the pursuit of pleasure. That's why the night has been an important source of wonder, thrill and revolt for many artists, writers and club kids. This goes beyond a Baudelarian sense of wandering the city and more towards embracing the nighttime as a time of play for grown folks. Just look around: at night, at the rave, at the party, the fashion is louder, skimpier, and more daring, and that's saying something loud and clear about the kind of space we work to create.

17.

The crushing reality of life under capitalism makes us numb, strips us of feeling, keeps us in debt, and the end result is that grown folks forget how to be in their bodies, are too tired by it all. Adult entertainment is a reminder to come out and play.

Dancing Lonely: Becoming Black, Queer, and Trans

Ev Delafose

Much of how Black queer life is imagined is through the language and imagination of community and communality. From Ballroom culture to raves to serendipitous encounters in safe and unsafe spaces, Black queerness is constantly rendered as a world—or many worlds—of sociality. How then am I to consider my Black queerness when much of my existence is what I can only describe as *cold*? This essay traces a temporal collapse of my Black queer (dancing, voguing, raving) life where visual and sonic worlds lose their solidity and distinction and become amorphous memories. Subtending these memories is the aching, haunting breeze of cold-ness that serves as a reminder of the particular loneliness that follows Black queer youth through and to these events and spaces.

As a child, I dreamed of New York and of enjoying my body in motion with the other bodies of New York—the rumbling sub-way trains, the eclectic aesthetics of history shimmering along buildings, and other Black queer and trans lovers and dancers.

I danced to rap, hip hop, and R&B and their respective club and "vogue dramatics" mixes. As a twenty-something-year-old living in New York, I find myself confronted with a revitalization of the loneliness I experienced in my youth—dancing alone to this music and these mixes. This realization brings to the fore another tension: The digital worlds provided to me by Internet archivists of Ballroom and of raves do not exist. The veneer of ease, of accessibility, of community is scraped away by the coldness on the dancefloor.

Cold on the Dancefloor

Flesh frozen solid by loneliness. At 2 a.m., there were two more hours left at this rave, and still, I felt the breeze of air conditioning command my hairs to stand. I began dancing around midnight, and still, I had yet to feel cloth, let alone skin, brush against my exposed shoulders or any part of my body. All I felt was the weight of the music suffocating me, and all I could see through the overwhelming fog was a blonde girl on her phone with a sparkling Fendi Baguette bag and (barely) white Air Force Ones. She stood there in the fog, like the hamper in the corner of my bathroom.

Peering through more of the fog, I could see a similar stillness all around me: a tall person tapping their foot, condensation torpidly trickling down my walls, a huddle of tall Europeans attempting to hold a conversation over the sternum-rattling sounds of KYRUH, my shower curtain rhythmically gyrating to the onslaught of running water. Of course there were many dancing as well because KYRUH's set was infectious, but I never felt the sweat that I could see flying on and off bodies in footage of Kaytranada's iconic *Boiler Room* set from 2013. Instead, everyone seemed to remain rather matte-skinned.

This recounting is not an indictment of raves or New York City, but instead is a realization of how digital queerness and transness, as unifying structures for their particular communities, produce fantasies which establish parasocial relationships and false realities that leave the (Black) queer in a shock of loneliness. Regarding the KYRUH set, it was not KYRUH, or the Europeans, or the blonde girl with her Fendi bag that let me down or tricked me into a false sense of community; it was the gloss of the virtual realms of Black queer and trans life that crafted an illusion of sociability. It was the fantasy worlds produced on the Internet where I lost sense of how the flesh—how the fleshy tongue—operates.

Leo Bersani explains that "the pleasure of sociability is the pleasure of existing, of concretely existing, at the abstract level of pure being."[1] However, since the publishing of the article "Sociability and Cruising" in 2002, the Internet has become a different entity, and the creatures born of this new entity are not being confronted with its mistranslations until quite late in life. Prior to explaining the pleasure of sociability, Bersani reveals how one can dissolve the loneliness of individuality: "renounce . . . the acquisitive impulses that draw us into groups."[2] What Bersani is explaining is that one must sacrifice the fantasy in order to experience that pleasure of sociability.

The problem at hand is the intractability of the fantasy produced via the Internet. As a creature of the Internet, I suffer from an amalgam of fantasies produced by the conjunctive force of neoliberal desire for self-optimization and the internalization of the desire of the digital Other. This is not to discount the power of fantasy or the digital Other, but it is important to comprehending the unrelenting loneliness that accompanies this transition from the online to the offline. The ease of transitioning online manifested as a million different iterations of my self—I became a white man, a white woman, a Black woman, a Black lesbian, a Black transfemme queer. Fantasy granted me so much knowledge and comfort in changing and exploring myself. However, to return to Bersani, these communities to which I claim to belong—Black, queer, trans—move at a distinct rhythm to which I have yet to adjust. This rhythm is the comfort of sociality, and an unrelenting hold on fantasy can sever one's synchronization: "We live rhythmically only if we renounce possession."[3]

The Fantasy Problem

Dissolve the fantasy; embrace the real. Since I was nine years old, memorizing the lyrics to "Itty Bitty Piggy" by Nicki Minaj and "How Many Licks?" by Lil' Kim, I've been planning for my life in New York City. Obviously New York in 2009 was drastically different than it is now, but the want never waned. Instead, it was around 2012 or 2013, when I learned about voguing and Ballroom, that my desire to live in NYC grew dramatically. In the bathroom while I let the shower water run, I would twirl my hands and swivel my hips to the great commentators of 1990s Ballroom videos. I would shake my phantom breasts like Sinia Azzedine Alaïa and whip my afro as if I were Amazon Leiomy Maldonado. I fantasized of being soft and cunt like Ricky Allure. So much of who I am is a coagulated embodiment of all of these names—from Nicki Minaj to Octavia St. Laurent.

How I came to be, then, was through a series of intimate parasocial relationships of motherhood and caregiving conducted by the digital personas or replicated imagery of these figures. To further articulate this parasociality, I want to turn to *Pose*, the television series. I recall the excitement, but I also recall a feeling of loss that washed over me. Parasocially, I lost something that felt like a bit of a secret, because the content I consumed consistently referred to and imagined Ballroom as an underground art form which was far from the truth by *Pose's* release in 2018.

After *Pose*, I began finding more and more videos of balls happening across the world, which struck fear into my plans for New York: Would I ever find my community in a community made up of the world? This question represents the naïveté of someone who has yet to comprehend, let alone align with, the subtending desire of a particular community to which they already see themselves as belonging. I spent a decade of my most formative years ingratiating myself into a digital community whose physical antecedent no longer existed. The underground where Sinia Azzedine Alaïa, Octavia St. Laurent, Leiomy Maldonado, and Ricky Allure were up-and-coming and making a name for themselves in the Ballroom scene no longer existed. There were balls in Russia, an Irish teenager teaching *Ireland's Got Talent* how to vogue, and the tragically iconic line by Vanessa Hudgens: "I'm so into voguing right now." Only recently has the naïveté slowly dissipated.

In September of 2022, there was an OTA—"open-to-all"—event run by Open To All Entertainment, which began hosting more accessible balls in 2019. It was not a particularly special ball. Barricades were now a common feature of OTA and balls of high volume attendance. Snookie Lanore, or Snookie Juicy West, was the commentator, and the category was "Performance with a Prop." After a few walks, Snookie exclaimed, "Y'all gotta clap!" Of the very few balls I have attended and of the many performances and balls I have watched online, I can't recall a commentator having to get a packed audience to be interested or responsive to the category at hand. Other than trying to get people to be louder, this phenomenon of disengagement seems to be one attached to the devices which capture our engagement. Now, as I say this, I recognize the function of recording balls, but there is also a severe dysfunction. Nearly all of my experience with Ballroom is mediated through recordings, and yet I find myself cringing watching ROSALÍA stepping out at an OTA in September and seeing nothing but a sea of cameras and flashlights. I don't intend for this to come off as an anti-tech, purist rant about how audiences' manners of engagement are terrifyingly disengaged. This recognition grounds a greater critique or interrogation of Ballroom and its foundations.

Interpolated over the iconic Ballroom track by Ellis D, "Work This Pussy (Hurt Me Mix)," in Teyana Taylor's "WTP," Octavia Saint Laurent gives a confessional, first seen in *Paris Is Burning*: "I believe that there's a big future out there with a lot of beautiful things. . . I want so much more; I want my name to be a household product." In *Queen of The Underground*, Octavia again states plainly: "I want to be a star, simple as that." Or as Venus Xtravaganza says in *Paris Is Burning*, "I would like to be a spoiled, rich white girl." These sentiments are repeated in shows and films like *Pose*, *Legendary*, *The Queen*, etc. At the foundations of Ballroom, there is aspiration and desire to be stars, statements, legends, icons, in and beyond the Ballroom community.

Celebrity culture, the foundation of the names of each house and names of house members, is instilled into the blood of Ballroom. Fundamentally, we can recognize the problem is a culture held captive by the standards of capitalism, and as Marlon Bailey says in his book *Butch Queens Up in Pumps,* "Ballroom members are neither interested nor able to dismantle the systemic forms of race, gender, and sexual hegemony that disenfranchise them. Rather, survival and the pursuit of a better quality of life are the aims of members."[4]

I want to think about the attendees of these balls. In *Pose*, the critique is practically spelled out as Evan Peters plays a character named Stan, a married, upwardly mobile white man who peruses the piers watching the trans sex workers. In the show he ends up dating Angel, one of the main characters, and is brought as a guest to a ball, a world he has never seen or experienced outside of the denigrating journalism which reports on these underground gatherings. Stan was and does represent a sector of those that consume and attend the balls—tourists of the underground, whether consuming out of love or out of fetish, who are voyeurs or admirers, perhaps both at the same time.

This is a sentence that terrifies me and my own worldview because of how I arrived to Ballroom. As I watch and share Ballroom videos, I see Stan filling the comments and the view count on some of the videos that functioned as formative documents for my development. Stan is that fetishistic, seemingly anthropological gaze manifested as the cisheterosexual white gaze cannibalizing the Other, the Underground. When it is not a policing gaze, it is this gaze, the cannibalistic gaze, one of pure, unadulterated consumption. The cannibal gaze consumes and pops out "Helicopter Hands" on TikTok—also known as "Figure 8" hand movements in voguing. The cannibal gaze consumes and produces what Leiomy terms as "Noguing"—choreographed, emotionless dancing that chews up and spits out practically AI-generated dances loosely based on voguing. The cannibal gaze proudly announces, "I'm so into voguing right now!" Moving to New York revealed the terror that I grew up in a community of ghosts and Stans, but similarly terrifying is the reality of Ballroom.

Balls are now littered with spectators rather than participants. Balls were collaborative study events where attendees collectively produced an archive of Black and brown queer and trans feelings, affects, performances, embodiments, and aesthetics. The Leiomy

Lolly hair flips, Sinia Alaïa's titty-shaking, Daesja LaPerla's light-ning-quick and sharp hands, Kevin Allure's shimmy dip, soft and cunt. All of these became part of the Ballroom lexicon that the great-est performers studied. Today is not void of legends either: Eyricka Lanvin's posing, Gravity Balmain's boneless, yet angular hand and floor performances, The Princess of Philadelphia, Makayla's stunts, Honey Balenciaga's catty dramatics. The archive grows, and yet its guardians seem to be missing from the audiences—or at least are pushed around by the tourists. Perhaps it's the oversaturation—too many balls, too many performers, too little time in a society where spending time not making money is almost equivalent to spending money itself. So, the fantasy must dissolve where we must survive.

This is where this cannibal culture, as mediated by camera-equipped devices, gives something back. I cannot imagine my life without eleven-year-old me spinning and dipping on tiled bathroom floors, trying my damnedest to be quiet, while still being *cunt*. As a consequence of much of my research into Ballroom and trans communality, I've come to fall in love with holding the tension close to my heart: the tensions of a consumptive, anthropological gaze and the necessity of maintaining Black queer and trans archives and (hi)stories.

I grew up in the deep South with relatively strict parents, so when it came to my queerness and my transness, I could not find that com-munity, that kinship. I ate what I could find. I consumed everything. Even if I am only recently finding myself inside of it, Ballroom was the only place I could find a home. So, I am grateful to Noelle Archives, iamsugarchampagne, Jay Garçon, Ballroom Throwbacks Television, Streetstar and all of the other guardians and platform-ers of Ballroom, voguing, and its cultural workers. These archivists are reaching every iteration of my child-self—the Black, queer and trans children trapped inside in an unwalkable city stuck facing a screen with headphones in.

Kill Your Darlings

Black gay time space.[5] Black queerness and transness function to undermine the white cisheterotypicality that defines much of the World as we know it. Hester Baer, in discussing cyberfeminism, explains that "discourses of privatization and individualization that prevail in neoliberalism transform 'systemic projects of resistance into commodified private acts of rebellion,' undoing insurgent feminist knowledge and counter-hegemonic feminist politics."[6] As much as I levy critique against Ballroom, the community, and the voyeurs, I recognize exactly how one can internalize and succumb to the fantasy of optimization, perfection, beauty, and celebrity. Now, at the juncture of fantasy and reality, there is a suffering.

I hear my bathroom door rattle with anger because I danced too long and let the hot water run out. I feel that breeze of air conditioning snake its way down the back of my shirt. I see the aching members of Ballroom constantly seeing how celebrity culture consumes and elevates a select few, but it cannot save us all. In all of these moments, loneliness and disappointment freeze us in place and ask us to reconsider our fantasies and sacrifice the very thing that drew us to the physical worlds, these realities. As much as I wish to dance alongside the sweaty bodies at Honey Dijon's 2018 *Boiler Room* set or press against the back of someone trying to get the best view of Daesja Laperla's iconic hands performance with a prop in 2004, the fantasy must dissolve so that I can find my way into reality and find these moments in their material forms, rather than digital. Time will collapse; it is how Black queer and trans life operates, so I must live in Black queerness and transness and disrupt the linearity, the white cisheterosexuality—the fantasy.

Entertainments of the Moment

Afsana Mousavi

1.

She goes to work. She washes the dishes. She gives herself her shot. She sits on the edge of her bed, forgetting. She goes to work. She hits her vape. She changes her name. She looks at her phone. She will call this the first transsexual summer of her youth. She goes to work. She goes to her neighborhood's infamous dive bar, in an old church on the corner of the street. She keeps thinking the night will offer something to her, an amalgam of thinly imagined anticipations and misremembered tropes, daydreams of pomp and eros awash on a shore of panic; often she is disappointed, misguided, straining towards enjoyment like a Midtown gay wearing an unevenly cropped t-shirt and rainbow shorts on Pride weekend, his sour sweat still in the seams when he tries selling it to the thrift store where she works.

She gets invited to castings. She considers boys. She returns at night to these dives. She goes to Le Bain, at Kat's request. She and Kat had met at a reading by a dark-humored faggot who was enjoying something like mainstream success in the twilight of his cynical life. Or if not mainstream success, then people in New York were tweeting about him.

Io had known of the writer for some time but put off picking up his work; when she first saw the re-edition announcements (retweeted by someone she admired who was obliquely related to a publishing house she adored) her body responded physically. There is an element of speed to living that she just can't quite grasp. One must be intimate with the city's delusions in order to survive.

After the reading, Kat and Io bonded over their obsessions with all the same things, namely dense, academic texts touched by thrill and devilish reputation, a rebelliousness approximate to *cool*. Both Kat and Io had recently moved to Bushwick and both found new service-industry jobs (but the boutique kind) and both would soon leave the cyborgs and gender terrorists of such writing behind, settling into a more sober commitment to pleasure, making-do, and in Io's case, transsexualism.

At Io's new job hardly anyone is over thirty and everyone does something else, swishing in Japanese tulle and ornately pleated polyester, tabis and selvedge denim. Someone was Nan Goldin's assistant; someone is in talks to do something with Elena Velez. She clocks in. "I'm so hungover." "I came straight from the afters." "My heart won't stop racing. I'm scared. I hate drugs." Cicadas in the heat and the wet, their chirrups turning over through the rafters, the morning.

She and Kat step off the L, clicking over the cobblestones and desolate glass of the Meatpacking District on their way to Le Bain. Io is skeptical because she has heard from her new coworkers that Le Bain is dead. She has a sickness about her, the kind of cold, calculated observation true weak people nurture to best pick out the desirables and fit in. Io is wearing a black see-through Rick Owens dress, black Margiela heels several sizes too small, a little black purse, thong. Blue eyeshadow she is going to hate when she looks back on selfies in less than a year. Something about Kat and Io is similar. Less looks than movement, beginning in one and ending in the other.

The line is round the block, a Manhattan line: short girls in skinny jeans bereft of composure, their Kate Spade purses touching the sidewalk. Io gives up immediately. "Walk," Kat tells Io, so Io walks. "No. In front of me." She squeezes Io's hand and pushes her ahead. Kat recognizes something that Io will only pick up on much later. Kat is from outside LA; she has developed a sensibility, culled from zines, experimental music, CalArts, an ailing once-actress mother, stories of swingers and airplane-part factories. (In Io's past: Texas gas station, Costco on Thursdays, dragonflies plunging over the faraway. There is so much wind here even stones go blank, as Ovid said.) Kat can suspend her disbelief, she knows how to work the residue slapdashery leaves behind.

Cut the line. In. Io pointedly ignores the trans woman working coat check; if she looks she will be lost. She sees herself with painful clarity—the estrogen having had no impact yet—the face still set in hard lines—the stiffness of the comportment—she's roe. A great and terrible elevator, like the machinery the mind populates sleepscapes with, brings them up. The space leaves no impression.

Minutes after arriving a man walks up to Io and tells her she's hot. They make out. Dick gets hard—the one attached to Io—it's not exactly arousal, it's like her feet hurting. He says I don't have any condoms. She says Okay, he says Well can you suck my dick at least, she says Okay. He says Let's go to the bathroom, she says

Okay. She has heard about this, in books, anecdotes, memes, but she can't believe how quickly it's happening for her, that all it takes is a dress, how simple the codes are, almost brute. The truth is men love trans women because they like the idea of fucking the boy out of a boy. It's no different than dogs humping one another, almost desireless, it's about the minute experiences of power's lusty and banal dregs. There's real thrill to that, this is no judgment. This is Manhattan, so of course there are bathroom police. Aw, Io maybe says. Feigning dismay.

And something something something. She spends most of her time elsewhere, only occasionally cutting across the edge of the dancefloor. A change is passing through the music, a tempo or an intent, soundless like Io's dilating pupils. Kat is leaving for the airport. "Here," she says and puts her ketamine in Io's hand. Io has to bend down to be eye-level with her. Kat leans in, her hair sticking to the high color in Io's face, she kisses her cheek. She has known Io by a different name, when Io wandered in a yellowing tank top stained with fake blood, let her happy trail grow unruly and wore low-waisted jeans to show it off. Broke, smoking Newports they found on the ground, going to the East River instead of eating.

That look in boys' eyes. Kat has watched Io make the hardest choice, the most humiliating: to live. Later Kat will move back to California for grad school and they will fall out of touch. Privately Io will think of her as the last vestige of her cis existence, as part of one of the upright, the daylight; an eddy before her life disappears into itself, before every latent element, every effect obscured beneath her experience, suddenly assembles with the intensity and merciless timing of a militant force, all at the expense of everything she has taken to be recognizable. Never before, she would think, and possibly never after have I undergone such upheaval. And that girl

I was, she gave herself over to it, simply, blankly, without mourning. I admire her for that; I could not do that now.

Paul Virilio said that what happens is so far ahead of what we think, of our intentions, that we can never catch up with it and never really know its true appearance. Or maybe that was Sophie Calle. Music coming into itself. The track usurped by a different unit like pinched matter released from its own tension, ripples spreading, vanishing. Our still-breastless girl watches the night slowly pull back from the skyline. Of views and prices she prefers the M train as it turns on its tracks between Myrtle-Broadway and Knickerbocker.

Before she can really decide to leave, two friends of friends text her from downstairs. The party is at capacity. Very drunk she gets into that livestock elevator. She still drinks, she hasn't yet fully accepted the powder into her life. What compels her bluff, how does she know to walk up to the bouncer, very prim, very arch and with a lip curled? She says, "Those are my friends. They're supposed to be on the fucking list!" He grabs her friends from the teeming crowd of misfortunates. This time she glances at the trans woman working coat check, who cuts a knowing smile her way. Io prickles with something: excitement, anxiety; she wants to wipe the smudges off the air between them, but the elevator is opening and one of her friends is grabbing her by the wrist, saying "That was just like *Euphoria*."

Io will wear the memory smooth, the bouncer taking in her transvestism. She cannot imagine that he was also seeing her whiteness.

She drifts from the friends of friends. Going nowhere, looking at all that has been given up, crowd disintegrated into polyps. Io is skirting the dancefloor just as the last DJ takes the booth. Statuesque, forehead tattoo and lip gloss, rippling with—what—Io doesn't have a word for it—*gorgeous*, *sexy*, *hot*, these terms seem dated, gimmick. Io feels her in her phantom tits, in her flesh's memory of what it should be. When she was a boy at punk shows she jumped up and down, shook her head; it was feet and skull. Now her body releases the gaminess of itself, responds with ass, with an arched back, flourishes shaking off the mechanical encrusted on the masculine.

Svelte, trancey techno, and there's such sentiment at its edges. It hits Io hard like waking up from the possible, not a dream not a nightmare but the sense of it so striking she's hooked, each beat landing like *I wish I could sleep for-ever.* Her transsexual feet cry out in the Margielas. Mostly she's thinking about how embarrassing she must look. She closes her eyes to forget but the DJ remains, her hair her gloss her tits. And from their turning their backs on time comes a hint of the familiar, an endless, yawning reverb, the bubbly synth of Io's favorite Arca track. These things are here for Io to read the personal into, a flush of recognition from what is life-less—chance or God maybe. All of her beliefs disappear.

She is alone. She longs for sense to give way to celluloid, for the repetition of the cinematic. Movies don't really end. Something else happens, mysterious, intractable. The images take flight.

2.

They tore down that one factory did you hear—Remember—That one night—Before the pandemic—

It's Eva speaking, one of the coworkers that Io finds herself thrilling at the sight of. Something about the Galliano bags and the halo dyed into Eva's hair and the way she completely ignores Io, at times even actively ensures that her shifts are worse than they have to be, but Io still finds herself eavesdropping, transfixed by the sleepy longing that has softened Eva's otherwise veneered beauty. I think it was *Unter*, Eva is saying, Vanessa was still around then—I wonder where she is now—We were other places before—For days after everyone was blowing this black soot out of their noses—It was so cold—I lent that incredible Gaultier top to Vanessa—It was the most irradiated spot in Brooklyn—When we woke up it was night again and my Gaultier was gone—She'd worn her Tabis and one was by the door and the other was in the hall—Completely destroyed—

It has a power over Io, this story, this reckless girl. She imagines motes of radioactive fungi falling slowly over the revelry, tracing bioluminescent spirals that shiver when buffeted by the trembling subwoofers, she imagines trying on Eva's dreaminess herself, in the future, that dreaminess which is native to recollecting the nights out of one's past, a dreamy awe which can be read like the history of the city itself . . .

Walking home after work one night a car screeches onto the sidewalk. A woman, the impossible kind, holds a container of strawberries out the window and pours water over them. Her acrylics. The bass. The falling water catching the streetlight. Summer.

With Brooklyn Io finds an unforgiving apprenticeship to the luxurious entertainments of the moment. ThriftBooks' throne in the sugary repository of her reward circuit is supplanted by SSENSE. It's nice to love living more than having a mind. She is twenty-two. On Tinder she matches with a boy whose attractiveness sends trills of malaise low in her stomach. She looks up from their texts and her eyes are empty of the real. He comes over. He is withdrawn afterwards. Her face is sticky, carpet-burned, odiferous and dreamy.

Later one of his mirror selfies appears on her timeline, liked by accounts she follows because she thinks they are funny. He is wearing a t-shirt that says FBI: FEMBOY BUSSY INSPECTOR. Mindlessly, piloted by the macabre, she scrolls his account to see if he tweeted anything around the time of their tryst. There is one from the very night: *i think dumb people are hot.*

Most of Io's days are cast into flou by a giddy sense of the inexorable, a naïveté that only sometimes is fast enough to cover over the ignominy beneath. She goes to work. She goes to the rave. She goes to work. She goes to work. She complains to her coworkers about the taking of Ethel Cain by the faggots and the nonbinary cis girls. She hits her vape. She goes to the rave. One of her coworkers is DJing. She knows them as Junya, but here they are DESTIERRXXX, and their set crashlands amid the city-hardened bodies in the crowd, softless bodies flung, movements like debris. The long, singular loc at the base of Junya's neck is tucked under a sleek blonde wig. Comme de Garçons on top, Kiko Kostadinov on bottom, and lit up by a witchy sexiness, the kind of masculine beauty Io grew up thinking suspect, she thinks of inverts, perverts, the miraculous kind of hedonism associated with that lot, and then Junya cuts in the bloodhungry alarm from *Kill Bill*, mixing it with a slippery chant in a language Io can't identify, she's pinned to the unlikely pairing by a beat both hard and supple, motile, someone tries to pull her away to do coke but she shrugs them off, her presence on the dancefloor has a breathless precarity she likens to chance, I can't believe it's me here I can't believe it's me here, the uncertainty heightens her enjoyment to something almost malevolent, I can't believe it's me here I can't believe it's me here.

Next day she's two hours late to work, arrives just as Junya's Marsèlls are stepping down from an Uber. "Girl—," Junya screams. "Girl," she screams back.

Duration shrivels, distills, turns inward, is lit up by a general appreciation for what is of itself. Each night out, each cluster of magazine color she takes in, the investments in her future that have guided Io come undone. Academia is no longer the most engrossing proximity to ongoing life. She measures everything against the speed of light hitting her flesh; the fuller pensiveness she understands as required for writing becomes awkward, unsustainable.

When she writes, if she writes, it is in her NotesApp, naked clauses, words she likes, description to take her experiences from pure to tangible. Sometimes, dreams. In one, a poem. She's lucky; she's not like Orpheus; she gets to bring some of it back with her.

It 4.

It go [. . .]

Since when did dancing to the same disc at the backend of 3 a.m. become a rave?

[. . .]

My hair falls, hot and untouched, finally in pace with me, to sleep.

Fragments barely recovered from the blistering hardcore of night's other kingdom. Perfect for their disrespect of time, their bitchy I-know-a-thing-or-two frustration, and their intimation of that final taste of expenditure, when Io is in bed after a good rave, and the AC kicks on, the building responding to the heat her body throws off as it slowly turns acids into sugars.

A glut for the idyll etcetera of life, she discovers Lauren Berlant, Miss Deanna's knitwear for Margiela, Honey Dijon, *Sweet Days of Discipline*, TS Madison, *Desperate Housewives. . .* She learns the parlance. Kundle. Carry. Giving. Tore. Words taken from whom, and deployed to what end? She does not like to answer that question. She uses the phrases which denote the sensations shared across bodies in the night, bodies that happen to be hers. This lexicon—tricky, seductive—is nevertheless touched by a fine line, across which her place could only be mimetic in the basest sense, devoid.

Dragged it. Dragging it. Gathered. Gagged. Cunt. *Cunt*. At last Io has something to describe that closer DJ from Le Bain. She scrolls the club's Instagram, finds the flyer for the party, scrolls the tags, guesses at the names, finds that DJ's account. Couture. Just Couture. Like Colette was just Colette. She's so cunt it's heart-stopping. Bed-bound, Io blinks in the screen's light, drunk on the artificial deprivation of melatonin. Couture's tits are huge, perfect, the tits you dream of, a dream not made of mud and unwilling to return to dust. In one image Madonna puts her face in them. In another Io traces the tattoos that edge their inner curves from where the ink spreads over her sternum. Large, expensive-looking tattoos, dragons, chains, delicate and vegetal growth, all a soft blue that plays at being black.

It was on her phone where Io first started registering oblique glances of her generation of trans girls. Shaved eyebrows, dark eye makeup, the languorous bravada and sultry candor of Black ballroom queens walking realness in the late '90s and early aughts picked up by girls barely out of their teen years and already orbiting print magazines, runways, the venues she's always seeing on Instagram flyers. This term—*doll*—floats around, girls fight over it, its origins; faggots join in for no apparent reason. PhDs quote-tweet. The replies are full of DJs and sex workers. She walks down the street with her headphones on and the afterimages of the discourse pouring senselessly in and out of the back of her mind, they teem, light as air, the moment she arrives at her destination they will be gone and she will not even remember them.

Turning corners or crossing doorways her gut catches with commingled dread and anticipation, she searches the people in the room, doesn't know who she's looking for. New York is a landscape of anonymity, chance, doppelgangers. On the subway, an ad sponsored by the NYC Department for the Aging: *Ambition is ageless.* At twenty-two the possibilities for Io's life are no longer endless. DJ. Sex worker. Model. Writer. Tech. Retail. Eventually, apocalypse. There is only so much a tranny is allowed to do. If she moves fast enough she can forget. At twenty-two her legs are already marked by odd lumps, misshapen veins forced against the inside of her skin from working jobs where she stands all day.

She scrolls Couture's account again. Then, again. Her bio says NY/BLN. She's in a large bed with Couture, the mattress flat on the rug, up against a series of steel windows, just their heads peeking out of the furred coverlet, and outside it is the timeless, milky light of winter, when small sounds fill whole rooms. The image is there behind Io's eyes and then gone. It lacks the touch that diffuses the shock of sex. She stands with her mouth open and thinks of it, an approaching train tugging at strands of her hair, her clothes.

3.

Junya lists her for their *Fourth World* set at Basement. They also list Eva and Kiyo. Of her coworkers, Io lusts over those three the most, a chaste lust, the lust of wanting else. She accepts this information with numbness, a small smile. Tentatively, she allows herself to believe the nervous asides about Glissant and Kawakubo she directs at Junya over hours together in the fitting room might have accreted to something like friendship.

"Don't mention anything about list to anyone," Kiyo tells her in passing. Dust lies on the concrete floor beneath the tepid morning heat. July ferments, pressurizes the air, montage of pull-tabs cracking color-streaked cans, caffeine stiffening the service laborer's skin. "Why?" asks the ingénue, taking a plug from her mate. Kiyo doesn't look back, says, "People will get their feelings hurt. Junya only had a few list spots."

Io drifts to the supply closet-cum-breakroom. Absently, she runs her tongue over the filmy sweetener coating her teeth, flung by the grotesqueness of victory, her supremacy. She fantasizes about nightlife the way cis women fantasize about marriage. Lifting her hair she positions herself in front of the fan so as to cool the delicate vertebrae at the base of her neck. She texts Junya. "Who else is on the lineup? Sooo excited. Tysm." They send back a screenshot of the flyer. Couture.

The morning gives up under the afternoon. Nowhere in that part of Bushwick is cheap, so Io walks instead of eating. The afternoon turns over to rain. There is a small park with trees that overhang its fence. A funereal dust tints the air, slightly green. The city quiet. The air hazy, warm, convalescent. Couture. Colorless spiders the size of grains of rice shake from the branches, spin out on invisible lace. They land in Io's eyes. Tiny, livid bites on her wrists. The skin tightens. She leans against a tree, as if winded. Bark presses her aching chest. Her forehead is clammy. Unimaginable, the satisfaction of the envious.

4.

That first summer called post-pandemic, an urge to bluff descends on all those who dream in cognitive vocations, those who can transmute look, language, recognition into dentist appointments, Whole Foods, good credit. Each time Io sees an announcement via Instagram post or a byline on Twitter she secretly feels betrayed by life, a doomy sense of her own weakness. With the desperation of the young transsexual she catches up on PC Music, Lyme disease, Staff International—then pretends none of it was ever unfamiliar. She toys with being in-the-know. She tries to name what she sees, treat her sensations as vanguard. According to her the vibe is pale-olithic chic. If she says it with enough confidence it really does register in her body as a prickling hint of premonition.

Io ties a sheer black scarf haphazardly over her sore chest, then knots a scrap of something around her ass, finishes off with Rick Owens FW2016 Cyclops boots and a ragged shearling pouch that hangs off one shoulder. She moves with a thousand ghost images filleting her mind, left ajar for the feminine and the qualitative to leak into mismemory. When she looks in the mirror she almost sees one of the beings that limn her ravelife: tall, skin, hair, need. She sees a hint of what it could be like: the delicacy of taking the contemporary into the body.

For a moment Io sits on the couch in her apartment, silent, with the hideous orange light and the broken ashtrays, silent, staring at nothing, at how she lives. Then she does a line of molly, calls an Uber, gets to Basement. Kiyo and Eva are already somewhere inside. She gets in line. The middle distance falls out of itself. "I'm on DESTIERRXXX's list," she says. T-girls get in free regardless, but she has the even more distinct pleasure of being listed specifically. Something venal in her terribly satisfied.

There's a girl standing colt-like in the middle of the lot. Denim mini-skirt, dewy skin, Adam's apple. Io recognizes her from the Grindr feed; when she applies the *trans* tribe, their little cubes are always relatively close to one another. She'd even messaged Io once, when Io was still a boy. They lock eyes and the doll smiles. She says, "Your hair looks good." She says "Have a good night girl," with an oblique emphasis on the word *girl*.

On the way in Io runs into an indie publisher she knows through a coworker, runs into someone she always sees on Instagram, runs into a dealer she can never tell if she's attracted to or not who practically forces a mountainous bump of coke up her nostril, then someone else, then an ex-academic who has just walked for Balenciaga, the show at the stock exchange. The ex-academic is also trans, older than Io, she always wants Io to work harder than she feels like working.

Once over lunch she'd told Io, "You don't have to be a doll you know." Wow she thought. True she thought. But it just seems like the most useful genre to orbit. Even so something chafed during her brief run-in with the doll in the miniskirt, that moment of recognition. It hurts to be slotted into heterosexuality like this, to move from the gaze of potential desirability to the scrutinizing gaze, but what a dream we'd all like to believe is true: that our social roles, especially where they are inflected by gender, could ever be inhabited without ripples of discontent. Not even transition can save you from that.

Zigzagging through the spectral obstacle course of people she sort-of knows, Io is sick with nerves, which are actually just her need, pulsing awake: to be inside, in the crowd. And then she's there and that instant when she's still only approaching the life clotted in shifting arrangements around Junya at the deck, that forgotten blip of time when she's crossing the sparsely populated patches of concrete, ever-thickening miasms running off the crowd like foggy membranes, that interval in which she sights the tight configurations closest to the booth—where she always stakes a claim, she loves to see the extraterrestrial light behind the DJ's eyes, sweat funneling off their lashes—and pulls her shoulders back, that instant stretches and billows out to the back of her mind, the rest of the glial cells in her skull given over to temperature, molly burning through her nerves, the flutter of consciousness Io retains is ejected, shot like a distant flare into the surround, crepuscular and suspended inside that approach-before-contact which remains draining off into daily time in perpetuum.

And Junya's set breaks over the crowd like dread come true. There's a look on their face like aggression, as in those numb moments one half-recollects after a fight, was there an open window, was the light that brilliant, was that really me who relished doing those things? The mix is saying Put-Your-Back-Into-It-Girl, demanding from Io her body, her work, her sex, and she hands it all over. She is put to work, a different kind of work, an expenditure of excess, working the real of her, the suet the pelf the delight of her, building pillars of salt. Junya cuts the beat and the crowd screams out in pain. It's not often in life one meets someone who understands what each of us secretly needs: to be tormented.

In her mouth she tastes someone else but it's just her own hair, she's sucking the crowd's sweat from where it has settled and soddened the pores of her hair. Junya's set yanks at the place where soapy alkali meet fat, saponifies, she imbibes mere matter. When she sucks on her hair she sees high color descending behind her eyelids even though her eyes are open. A hint of the social patters her sensorium and she spits the lock of her hair out realizing she probably looks crazy. Then it's streaks of the protein and the ventricle again.

The sound, the chemical. Pummeling Io into memoryless pas-
sages. Gestures that disappear into the night. She is outside sitting
on rocks or something. She keeps handing out gum to people. She
doesn't know when she got here or where the gum came from but
she knows if she stops to think about it something agile and necessary inside her will die.

As the darkness drains into morning she gives out molly to anyone
who wants some. Sighs. Coos. Before the flies are even buzzing,
before the flies have been pushed by the heat into that place they,
as all creatures, share with us—awake, wakefulness, supple where
the world impresses itself. Someone—her eyes focus, it's Kiyo—
tells her that Couture is on inside.

Lucidity shrapnels through the fugue. Io can hear Couture through
the walls, a 6 a.m. set, it sounds like the lights you see behind your
eyes when punched in the face. A creamy terror immobilizes Io.
Shadows pulse along their edges. She tells Kiyo to go on ahead,
then, when Kiyo makes a questioning face, motions at the rap-
id-fire conversation she's having with Junya. You know when you're
really high, she tells Kiyo, and you don't want to do anything but
stand in different rooms and talk really intensely and look around
and shit. "And," she says, leaning into Kiyo's ear while Junya talks
as if her attention hasn't broken away, "that one guy is still staring
at me. He keeps getting closer. That one, over there. No, that one.
Ew no what the fuck? Okay you're actually shady boots for that.
That one. Over *there*."

What she loves most is leaving the rave, that solitary walk home, sat-
uration sinking into the warehouses, blissed, blistered, pupils blown-
out, the sudden glimpses of residential idyll, a facade painted phtha-
lo-blue, birds with their soft bellies giving themselves dirt-baths, or

the weaving of a chain-link fence holding the purple smear of day-break like the city taking the morning into its mouth. An earnest love but one nevertheless fleshed out by the mammalian pleasure of being the right person in the right place at the right time: Io loves the zeitgeist, loves her inclusion in it, imagines herself as recipient of a stranger's yearning when future generations circulate glossy proof of this time. Walks of clemency, the reel of her life running through her mind like hyperpop, the same speed and glisten and evanesce, her life gone, she is alone, she has no support system, she hasn't been to the dentist in years, with few exceptions the people she has made staples in her life since moving here now seem remote, misguided, embarrassing. She is seeing her present memory for the last time in her life; with sweetness she detaches from it.

5.

—whirl, churn, fruition, empire longing for a dream of itself, cease-less as it gluts the etcetera of life, and even in the midst of denial and disbelief at its own heatdeath—as it glares, betrayed, with sullen reproach, at the impassivity of time—never attaining that dream, its perfect echo chamber—

6.

When he fucks her this smell comes out, not exactly of earthly life, almost ozone. Her socks are knee-high and she won't take them off because she's afraid she has boy feet. Exhaustion mutilated to resemble passion. While he's roiling inside of her he grips the socks and yanks. I don't care he says. She almost loves him right then. A fatigue that could be sweet, reluctant. They fall asleep with their bare boy-feet pressed together, worn and alive.

She won't care that she missed Couture's set until fourteen hours later when she wakes up, and he doesn't look as cute as he had before, now there's something a little scary about him, a little strained (as if he isn't unfamiliar with a girl named Tina—and a little too faggy besides)—even in sleep, when boys are supposed to look best, the terrible and, perhaps, unspeakably familiar hunger behind their features shut off. Those sleepy, downward-sloping eyes some boys have, big lips, like the testosterone is melting his face.

Her room is lofted, four floors of heat rises, when she moves his hand from her stomach she practically has to peel it off, and a sticky smell emanates from where their flesh was fused. She looks at her naked toes and it's that same old hatred, in the evening there is sex and in the morning there is hatred, except the evening was morning and the morning is afternoon. Io isn't sure anymore if he'd enjoyed the girl of her enough to disregard her feet. He might have been seeking out exactly her long, block-toed boyness. And she knows that when he wakes she will have to fuck him again, suck him again, and the sour taste in her mouth will be nothing but her own.

The windows are slats, close to the floor. In the underwater light she imagines him saying insane things to her. Really it's just her talking to herself. Is this how dolls taste. I thought dolls are supposed to be plastic. What kind of doll gets hard like this. Doll. Doll. Doll. Doll. This need ionized by glitz and tuck, an adhesive for the wicked and the fey. Doll. Doll. Doll. Doll. For her it is not a category or an identity but rather an associative mass, unearthed from the trimmings of her perceptions, a lifelong registry of sidelong glances, they shimmer behind her eyes, they layer, begin to accrue a weight, collapse in on themselves, it is almost like a panic, a voluptuous panic. Doll. Doll. Doll. Doll. It comes at her in big bold letters, like the need for clothing, which is the need for skin, for sex, for couture, for Couture, she's thinking of Couture. Her body, her life. She's pulling from her; pulling at her. As a doppelganger would pull at the form of its like. Flesh to flesh, guise to guise. She pulls as if at the handle of a doorway. She doesn't want to go out; she wants to get in, to get into living, into the green room—

Io sees her there. Couture sits, legs crossed, on a large couch, wearing a skirt the size of a belt but somehow still with no bulge. Her hair shines, it's as flat as a blade. There, Io says, stumbling towards her. Before this Io has been with someone, people, they all look good, keys of ketamine, she laughs and her voice is the kind of deep that makes Couture glance at her, this girl who still looks close enough to a boy for Couture's heterosexuality to snag. There is, Io says again. Couture looks up at her. She is wearing the Balenciaga sunglasses, huge, the shape slick and severe. There is a dream I come up against, Io repeats. Smiling, Couture finally responds, There is a dream I come up against again and again, and Io sits next to her. Io doesn't feel anything inside, no fear, she cannot die. Her knees touch and her feet are spread far apart. Girls, long legs. Smooth, hairless legs. They keep talking. Couture laughs, her dark head falls back. There is a dream I come up against again and again (a wall) There is a dream I come up against again and again (a wall), she says, and her voice is different. Io just looks. Couture helps her stand. There is a dream I come up against again and again (a wall) There is a dream I come up against again and again (a wall) There is a dream I come up against again and again (a wall), she says. There is a dream I come up against again and again (a wall) There is a dream I come up against again and again (a wall) There is a dream I come up against again and again (a wall) There is a dream I come up against again and again (a wall), she says. There is a dream I come up against. Again and again. (A wall.) There is a dream I come up against again and again (a wall). There is a dream I come up against again and again (a wall) There is a dream I come up against again and again (a wall). There is a dream I. Come up against. Again and again (a wall) There is a dream I come up against again and again (a wall) There is a dream I come up against again and again. (A wall.)

When the sun twilights at dawn

Jesús Hilario-Reyes aka MORENXXX

1.

"Our blur is a dancefloor at 4 a.m., that moment where in the crush of all-bodies lit up under strobes like firecrackers, we become no-body, and in the gorgeous crush of no-body, we become everybody." —Legacy Russell

Shimmering in a nightly disappearance
Folly, and intimately fragmented in fog
Enraptured, sacrilege of the self

As we exercise the gesture
In its vacant conviction of a matrimony
A precarious entanglement of terror and enjoyment can be . . .

Love as incandescent hate
Fogged up, breathed out of, poured into something hollow and yearning

An ocean floor—oceanic rave

Danced, gridded sea-foam and salted.
Cried out to fill this missing

"The dropout within techno and all other forms of Black musical composition speaks to the idea of the missing. . . On a deeper, deeper psychoanalytical level, what you're essentially hearing is Black people creating a universe within which that rupture, that loss that we are missing is fixed. Forcing an awareness upon us of what has been removed then taken from us. The missing, that thing we'll never find, never get back, never recover, it's speaking to that. The dropout is essentially a pulling away, an acknowledgment of a presence, an energy that has been removed from itself."—Elijah Maja on Arthur Jafa's *Theory of the Dropout*

the conscientious notion of filling a rapture
Disappearance as container, Shadow as container
Iconic lasers accommodate

Strobe lights bat their wings, like a blanket
Swaying wayward, antagonistic towards the waves
Pulsating, dying. . . slippery

It's gorgeous to witness, wildness come out of you
Has it come out of me? (*Or did you bring it to, and in and out of one another?*)

An eye roll glitches me into othered times,
Moments feel bent, submissive, and shivering
The shadow I just met sheathes around me, like a machete

2.
"Two bodies press outward from each other. The contact surfaces become a thing in itself. For a while, then it is over. For a

moment–how many beats?—this other dissociated state of enlust-ment. The enfolding bloom of lust, extruding out of bodies, toward each other. Detached from past or future; expanding into hot time. It's not like xeno-euphoria, into the cool otherness of xeno-flesh. It is into the sludgy banality of the mammalian body." —McKenzie Wark

Tornado . . . Cyclonic
Masses of flesh, woven and disentangling
Ritualistic field, montaging into contortions

Sexiness, Salination all over the floor
Corrosive, acidic-burning memory
Phosphorous enmeshed onto skins—embossed

The floor is beautiful like that, because of the violence
Amorphous and outside of
Brutal, as my swing is bewitching—

Murmurations awaken radioactive silt
As reds, and heat erode my porous neck

Blurring towards anything catastrophic
Gravity becomes necessary as it devils the spirit
Transient, Twisted, and fragmenting

"Disorder is our service, our antidote and anteroom, our vestibule without a story. We can't survive intact. We can only survive if we're not intact. Our danger and saving power is an always open door. Our venue is mutual infusion, the holy of holies in the wall, glory in a kind of open chastity, where the explicit body reveals itself demure in disappearance. Unenforced, slid, venereally unnatural and con-vivial, we claim slur against drill and document. Confirmation of the flesh is queer and evangelical." —Fred Moten

Dishonest dancers slur towards the horizon . . .
An attempt at the world, yet the floor becomes lava
And your limbs ecstatic and seafaring

Your body is a long black wing
Gently kissed by a curious wind, and itching with fervor
Thooming, as it folds to the beat

Extrasensory, as we are made to be folded
Salt lines our bodies and the air we share

The floors, maybe uneven too
Evidence, or the ground proves itself to become tomorrow

Repetitive mirrors, rotating on an axis . . . erecting lasers
Ribcages gyrate as bones are horny
This can be about sex . . . or impressions too

"I look at the dancefloor as a stage for queer performativity that is integral to everyday life. I am on the same page as Bollen when he considers the dancefloor as a space where relations between memory and content, self and other, become inextricably inter-twined . . . the dancefloor increases our tolerance for embodied practices. It may do so because it demands, in the openness and closeness of relations to others, an exchange and alteration of kinesthetic experience through which we become, in a sense, less like ourselves and more like each other. . . . In my analysis that does not mean that queers become one nation under a groove once we hit the dancefloor. I am in fact interested in the persis-tent variables of difference and inequity that follow us from queer communities to the dancefloor, but I am nonetheless interested in the ways in which a certain queer communal logic overwhelms practices of individual identity. I am also interested in the way

in which the state responds to the communal becoming" —José
Esteban Muñoz

Unfamiliarity hovers over like a hummingbird
Electric, Holy ghosted and dissonant

The frequency of the synthesizer sliced me to ribbons
Alien and unbecoming drone, earthquakes
This is working, the DJ demands so much of us . . .

Yet, I'm so easy . . . disarmed (even)
I'm directly in front of the booth, seductive
This transition feels like traveling—an archipelago

Immigrant, mapping and possible
My footing recovers like a diabolical wound, (*ancient*)

"Frequency is a sonic space [that] ranges from silence to deaf-
ening, dissonant noise; as a register of rapture and spirituality; as
a temporal feedback loop of memory, repetition, and renewal; as a
dynamic relation of call and response or chorus and verse; as a
haptic and kinetic space of contact and connection across the
African continent and its various diasporas" —Tina Campt

Finally, Flames dress you like a phoenix
The room has disappeared in the fog and the crowd has multiplied
Our ghosts' took ecstasy and danced beneath us . . . together

(Oh), she carried . . .
As if possessed, carving into the walls that vanished
To fill them with sediments and sand and meadows

Luckily, some of us have crossed the water . . . our thirst quenched
Or disowned

Liberation is not a space, but. . . maybe a sword
That comes . . . wet, addictive, and holding
Or maybe a storm . . . scorching, hazy and even blind

Death can be becoming . . . when documented
There is beauty, and remedy, and liquids amidst the blue light
you moved.

And we are all salty and decomposing
yet,
We couldn't be any further apart
When the sun twilights at dawn

You moved . . .

And so I ask again,
Will you take ecstasy with me?

Ghosts of the Dancefloor

Brittany Newell

Let's start with a joke.

What is the difference between an angel and a ghost?
Good lighting.

What is the difference between an angel and a ghost?
BPM. Angels like it groovy, smooth; ghosts like glitchy gabber shit.

What is the difference between an angel and a ghost?
A pill. The angel knew what she was taking in the gunky bathroom stall, the ghost didn't bother to ask and must suffer the consequences.

When I think about nightlife, the first thing that comes to mind is karaoke bars. Have you ever thought of karaoke as a form of benevolent possession? Letting our bodies be channels for the voices of strangers, often dead, always unreachable. So much of what we call nightlife is actually a way to make the immaterial material, to corporealize the vaporous or faint . . . thus a party is a séance thrown by winos, dykes, and skanks, each equally bereft. The ghosts knock on the table, spill a bottle of vermouth.

One more time. What is the difference between an angel and a ghost?

Proximity to a disco ball. Ghosts prefer corners, dark rooms, smoking areas crowded by bare-armed daddies who refuse to look cold. Meanwhile angels boogie towards the light, they didn't put on highlighter for nothing; anyone touched by the disco ball's light is suddenly sacred . . . behold the hallowed ground of collarbones.

Object lesson of a disco ball. An essay that I never wrote.

Lana sings: *Baby you, all the things you do, and the ways you move, send me straight to heaven . . .*

There's something mystic about a fog machine, both primordial and extraterrestrial, swathing bodies in states of pretty disarray. How nice to watch the body disappear, leaving behind only bracelets and teeth . . .

A gay bar dancefloor, one of the only places where exultation and decay coexist. The ghosts swish past, keeping us cool.

On a certain far-off dancefloor packed with sweaty bodies, I find myself awestruck by a wiry muscle-gay's expert use of his fan. You know, a big paper fan that he snaps to the beat, snaps to the beat. He fans the dancers around him and the sudden artificial breeze is like a miracle. I find myself thinking some people are simply anointed to know what to do with a fan in a crowd. But sometimes parties are like that: you look around and everyone is the sudden saint of something, no matter how grimy or low . . . Saint of the Gurn, Saint of Hard Nipples, Saint of Stupid Tattoos, Saint who Talks to You About Real Estate and Reality TV During Your K-hole, Saint of the Elderly Crossdressers, Saint of the Purple Plastic Miniskirt That Melts Upon Contact . . . . etc.

I encounter: two boys so heavily tattooed that their skin-color is indistinguishable (or is that the fog machine's trickery? Wreathing them in purple, blue?); they lock eyes with a devastatingly sexy man in a sweat-soaked wifebeater, his biceps like bread loaves, and they all three freeze in shock. Then they leap into each other's arms, laughing, crying, like long-lost lovers. When at last they untangle, one boy turns to me and says with tears in his eyes, *HE IS MY TATTOO ARTIST!*

Shall we contemplate the propulsive lack behind going out? The dancefloor as a space to get in touch with your holes? I stopped dancing once I fell in love. It's not quite true but it sounds nice. Dancefloor as a surrogate honeymoon, DJ as a Tall Dark Stranger repositioning your body to his liking . . . Lana sings *IF THS IS THE END, THEN I WANT A BOYFRIEND*, one of the best lines of twenty-first century poetry ever written. When I was all alone the dancefloor was my bedroom, as in a space to trash, get off, show off, have fun, be bad, that most private zone that we nevertheless allow strangers to enter . . . the dancefloor as a crowded bedroom, with bartender as witness.

Just like a dancefloor, a bed is always full of ghosts.

Then again, what defines a ghost? Ghosts come back from the dead because they have unfinished business. A party-dog is, perhaps, similarly consumed by their unfinished business, hence the compulsive need to go out at night, to seek heat, distraction, whatever . . . *TONIGHT IS THE NIGHT*, they scream, gussying themselves up. What are we waiting for, the final countdown?

Even in love, certain holes remain unplugged.

The most common human experience is to long alone. Sad music, electric blanket, the nubby pajamas your lovers don't see. Ready,

set, long. On a dancefloor longing is social, it's communal and gen-
erative. Like it or not, it's the reason for the season. Everyone's
flashing their broken hearts. I love the public hunger of dancing,
our need twinkling like Xmas lights.

Do you ever hear words in the bass, repeated like spells, in the
unsk-unsk-usnk, like extraterrestrial messages being transmitted to earth? On a certain dancefloor I heard GOD IS GOOD,
GOD IS GOOD; then GHB GHB; finally, SPIRONOLACTONE,
SPIRONOLACTONE. My dance partner says he doesn't hear it but
smiles politely and says, *May we kiss?*

I used to hear messages all the time in the bass at The Stud—
so what if we *were* receiving alien frequencies on the gay bar
dancefloor? I can think of no better space for the transmission of
Otherworldly Codes than this foggy purple plane, our bodies limps,
our boundaries weakened? Is that the party-dog's anointed task, to
be the recipient of different and sometimes challenging vibrations?
Or is it just to cheek-kiss and look sexy, which is, in my opinion, an
equally holy endeavor?

If I were to meet an alien I think they would look the way a synth
sounds. Stretchy, long, expansive. This is one of many drug-
thoughts better kept to myself. Such as: *hot girls have stuffed ani-
mals on their beds, this is a fact.* Or: *all horses have bangs, how
perfect is that?*

So we agree: A dancefloor is otherworldly. It is a site for temporary
lovers, past selves, forgotten futures, all layered together in a weird
tiramisu.

Lineup of party-dogs: Australian K-dealing crossdresser with C-E-
L-I-B-A-T-E tattooed across his knuckles. Never forget his smeared

table-top, the tropical plants in his bathroom that scared me. Moving on. Salome, who wore curtains to the club. Gina, with no underwear. Jackie, tracking steps. The little old man who drank heavy cream from a shot glass. An Italian twink who borrowed my lip-plumper and bellowed *BELLISIMA!!!!!* Is there any higher compliment than a fucked-up twink calling you hot? I think not. I tried to explain that the lip gloss might tingle or sting because of the lip-plumping toxins but he wasn't prepared. Oh well.

So many bodies I found beautiful, significant, and rare are little more than ghosts to me now. We grooved in tandem, that was all. And yet it felt like a revelation, a fogged intimacy.

Medical condition of a lip flip. Medical condition of a beat drop. Medical condition of a broken heart.

Bit by bit, we inch closer to heaven.

from CLUB SPACE

Anne Lesley Selcer

Joule tries to shadow a soft butch crab dancing low to the floor. I flirt with Tiger who leaves with Bunny. Between us is a heaven. It is Paradise's set. Everything starts when Joule puts their head on my shoulder. They have candy flipped and I am with Molly Bloom yes. It's hard to know who's on the inside and who's on the outside, whether the living bury the dead, or the dead bury the living. I have unfastened from belonging to anything but art, but when Joule puts their head on my shoulder, I come into the world. Because Aja is playing. I alight in tiger light, a lipstick bibliomancy, public sex for girls, I draw a red edge, everyone in this room is inside it. I bring Joule inside it. The music signals ecstasy to start, a whole holly sled with bells, we are together in the glee and weather, a thousand years of history present, instantaneously. All meaning is made here and left here, on the dancefloor.

This is not love. This is not sex. This is ecstasy. Black fingerless gloves, leather waist wrap. Girlish tiers of tulle. Cowboy hat, metallic skirt. Turbo boots with large buckles knee to ankle. Plaid skirt. Corset, posture collar. Large jacket, sneakers, loose tee.

Complicated primitivist mesh. Morticia dress. Schoolgirl skirt, black hair. White tee, dog collar, high platinum pony. Long black lace, black lipstick, a forehead jewel, heels. A bit of wire, and old rag of velveteen. A lion tamer's costume with diamond studs. A curling carriage whip and a fake revolver. A quill between the teeth, the aureole of a straw hat, a bunch of grapes dangling in one hand, the other holding a telephone receiver to one ear. A coin gleaming on the forehead, on the feet jeweled toe rings, ankles linked by a slender fetter chain. Scarlet trousers, jacket slashed with gold, white yashmak, violet in the night, leaving free only her large dark eyes and raven hair. Bloom: Molly!

At the club tonight I meet Xavier. I stand at the edge of the dancefloor in a pink bandeau bodice, laced up with pink rope. I am strawberry, bitchily commenting aloud as two men push past. They have disregarded my magnetic field with the dancefloor. Tall androgyne in onyx koala eyes, someone moving fast in ruffled kawaii, a black latex tank top, shy with short, bleached hair. The aqueous dancefloor is my gorgeous hydra lover. Xavier is suddenly next to me saying *wanna go dance* with lightness I receive as beleaguered exquisiteness, his sunrise smile wending into goth night. I learn he/they does not like men, they are trying to tell me their sexual preference, but I hear it as conspiratorial. The black shirt I've tucked into miniskirt, left back, is yanked by someone brushing past, "I'm flagging," I tell X., tongue out like a child's. I spot a swath of black mesh on the floor, pick it up, tie it over my eyes. I dance behind this reverse blindfold, watching Xavier's body dance. He throws vogue arms. I get consent and wind the mesh around his wrists. The dancing this lets out is astounding. He twists his wrists, shows them off, the energy is wild, aggressively hot. I dance behind, around, above, I make a space, protecting and enclosing my sudden new creature.

Sped into lowness, in the direction of the moon, it's always been best for me here, where flagellates and spermatozoa. The wind, the light, the noise of a sub-city, I am jacking a form of moving though time that is underneath bureaucracies of difference. I text Joule from the bathroom, *ecstasy is an eye that sees in all directions*. I fall to memory or reverie: I sucked my thumb, they fucked me from behind. I walked into the room, they were playing with the dildo. I kneeled and pushed it in with my hips, I slapped their face, I fingered their O ring. I sat atop the radiator to which they were handcuffed, I spread my legs as they looked up. They bit my nipples through my dress. I curled into them at the side of the rave, realized it would be our last, cried. They topped me like a boy, I squealed and shouted. I pushed them back on the bed, their head dangling over the edge, I moved up and down their c___, they caught their reflection in the half moon mirror I'd placed on the floor. They licked my c___, I said it was all I ever wanted. Just you and all the riches of the trees, almost anything will bend to you, you will bend to almost anything.

On the dancefloor, between the hours of 3 and 4 a.m. light radiates up her spine. All around her body, gold concupiscent rays. She is watched by the inviolate sun as a baby is watched by their mother. A nest of red is pulsating all ways around her head. She stretches out at the soft mouth of ecstasy. Now she is glowing golden. Gold travels outward, meets her perimeter and emanates, increasing her size. Her entire body slides over thick hibiscus. She is moving as if in seawater, caves of colored stones, eyes that flash. She pulls herself up onto the bank, legs flexed. "I love the shadow world more than thee," her one thought. A choir of aquatic plants give praise. Giant white lily pad flowers open slightly, she's hunting gently. She begins to climb, heroic in overcoming everything that is not pleasure. A dragonfly climbs higher than it's ever flied. All fauna and foliage is combed back and sated, sleepy and submissive as her feet return to the ground.

Between 4 and 5 a.m. a spontaneous piano staircase rises through the music, climbs up and over a waterfall. It flows like a rainbow from yellowed bright ground. The beat is seeking, a feminine melodica shaking hair from her eyes, sending morning up and out through a peephole. The scalloped rhythm of the coming day, the sun, fans of orange, huge phonograph barnacles flowering under water. We are being taken though by a woman's voice, she is guiding us. Small. Incompactable. Wrapped. Vaporous, metabolizing impactable. The curve of us flexes intricately around beauty, a lemon stolen from a tree. We are an acephale turned the other way round, to enter, with each other an idea which is a sound. Joule texts, femininity deincarnates the present. Each consciousness goes up and down. The sea is not messy. The moon is music. A curved ocean, yellow on green, blue striped, piles or pylons, an announcement to turn the head of sorrow, the sun has disrobed for us, we are inside the total withdraw of the visible, we dance, infinity squandered, dropped over the ocean like a library dropping into a pool.

Between the hours of 5 and 6 a.m. the sound is inside seaglass. The seaglass washes out with the tide, then comes back in a different color. All the rays of the sun, every single one, move through this room. Light projections on the radial ceiling slope over us where we dance. This beat sets the law as it builds, I am turned on by the illegality of change. I feel like crawling, some combination of a jaguar and a wolf, I'm in a plaid schoolgirl skirt and a black crop top. This beat is braying, then whining, then churning, this beat is losing, no never losing, but for a minute gets lost. Who is playing, bravely? Music is the objectification of time, I think in full words to later text to Joule, the thought riding atop a fully formed theory of change. Dionysus enters. I press my hands together, rub, stop at my solar plexus, project power outward, move them down, knees bent, hands together low, phallic. I become elephant, trunk to the ground, sensing. Then the music splits to butterflies, they escape around the top of my body. I have three heads in this sound. We are inside a terrarium of color.

Morning is bound at the waist by a tight plastic sash topped by two breasts caged in plastic, blue stockinged legs ending in tall blue platform shoes. She still wears the smudgy trace of the rose black ice lip gloss of night. She spits a silver wad of moon into the ocean. I step outside. My hair is in two French braids. O the fig trees in the Alameda gardens yes and all the queer little streets and pink and blue and yellow houses yes and the rose gardens and the jessamine and geraniums and cactuses yes. I come into day as if into form, the needle is no longer on the groove of my thoughts, my narrative is not delimited by the words I know how to say. I am called to the occasion of the sea which swallows the hot day in its foment of green, vaguely an age, vaguely a gender. In atmospheric drop, I'm a sailor coming back to land. Ridiculous, ancient. triumphant, invigorated by stupidity and sound.

Tonight I dress easily, tight under-bustier and opaque black tights. I step out at 12:15 a.m. and drive over the back highways and into the forest. This rave is thrown by girls. I flashlight my way down to the clearing: an animal skull mask, a latex leotard, a skirt over a skirt, two lovers, both with blonde braids. I dance behind them as they kiss, in my blonde braids I become their shadow, or their child, or their desirer, or them. *The feminine is a field of imagi-nation*, I text Joule in my mind. To be unmoored, to be attached to almost anything good enough. Dissolving like sweet fruit, I am alive in this defunded shape. I darktoe my way through bunchings of decorate, warm bodies, up the path to the altar. It is made of four levels of candles, votives at the base, eggs grottoed in, sprigs of baby's breath, a ceramic rabbit icon, a three tiered fountain with falling water. What are the vials? Estrogen. Every measure is linked to a form of power, I transmit to Joule. She thinks back, *sound teaches me the inconclusiveness of time.* We are celebrating Eostre. The next day will be the first warm one. The day after, the Spring Equinox.

Ecstatic Aesthetics: Mind Training on the Dancefloor

MX Oops

1. Shared Intentionality

You've already heard about the party, you know the vibe, but now you officially get the invitation, the flier, the community guidelines, a shared intention is forming.[1] With that in mind, you put together your look, rally the crew, and it's finally going down. You've made it through the line, past the door, and it's the first step onto the dancefloor; the smoke machine is only giving you three or four feet of visibility, the bass frequencies passing through your whole body, and syncopated lights invite the eyes to surrender. You are home.

Why do we gather? To get free, to feel better, to feel whole, and to complete the feedback loop of sharing energy and information with others that our nervous systems evolved to rely on. Our brains are born unfinished. Building new connections in the environment we are born into makes our incredible adaptability possible. This plasticity comes with a caveat, that we need each other to complete the puzzle of our developing consciousness. Human infancy is long compared to other mammals, and so in our evolutionary development, we evolved practices of *alloparenting*. Allo comes from the Greek term for other, meaning that a human infant may have several caregivers. For early humans to trust each other with offspring they had to develop an ability to guess others' intentions. Our bodies evolved the response of using our physiology to re-create a taste of other people's experiences to build a mindmap of their intentions.

We begin forming memories in the womb, our bodies remember the sensation of being both individual and at one with another and our environment. After birth, our nervous systems continue to refine the senses in response to the energies present in the environment; seeing for light, hearing for sound, and so on. The energy and information flow between us and other people flows through distributed mirror neuron networks within resonance circuits that support our relational sense.[2] We experience this when we feel happy when our friend is happy but we haven't heard the good news yet.

We are coming together to complete a built-in circuit for survival, repurposing it to generate a shared energy source, the vibe of the party. That energy support is useful because while "neurons that fire together wire together," a foundation of learning and memory in the nervous system, it takes energy for our bodies to create shifts in how we feel or in habits of perception. If you had a bad day at work, you might not be able to easily change your mood, but the party can be an energy source to get yourself back in alignment. The same process can be leveraged for more significant shifts in personality traits and personal growth. Evolutionary development has left us with features like a negativity bias that prioritized remembering negative experiences for increased survival. Thankfully, it has also given us the ability to use our conscious attention to shape and refine how we experience the world through our senses. While dominant culture reinforces a lone consumer-self separate from others, we have power. We can generate shared space through the accumulation of intentions that we bring into the space, and then manifest those intentions into the sweaty, fleshy, pulsing togetherness of the night.

2. Enriched Environments

Our brains are shaped through experience, through interactions with each other and with our environment. Neuroscientist Marian Diamond's experiments in the 1960s showed that enriched environments increased brain mass and neural integration in rats.[3] This idea of *neuroplasticity*, that the brain changes in response to environment and experience over time, was a pivotal shift from the paradigm that the brain only decays as we age. This was the first time there was empirical evidence that the brain is rewired through experience. Rats in environments with stimulation and frequent changes had larger brain mass than rats in environments with little stimulation or change. Enriched environments like the beautiful complexity of the forest or a thumping audiovisual installation in a packed warehouse can create positive stimulus for nurturing neuronal growth and integration.

In addition to enriched environments augmenting perception how we direct our awareness also influences the neuroplastic changes in the brain.[4] This is the dance of the mind, the emergent process that regulates the flow of energy and information.[5] How do we direct that flow toward integrative wellness? The dancefloor can be a place to regularly orient the direction of neuroplastic change. This might happen to varying degrees naturally, but if we are mindful of these possibilities the process is much more expansive. We can experience our senses more vividly and our relational sense of connection more deeply.

Using the energy of the party, you can cultivate a sense of inner connection, interconnectedness with others, and intra-connectedness within community. Integrating your senses, bodily sensations, and mental and emotional activity, can provide an inner sense of connection. Dancing together creates an opportunity to find an interpersonal sense of connection with the people there. This interconnection can also include a sense of *intra*-connection, where you feel that you are within an ecosystem of interdependence.[6]

These three layers of connectedness use the enriched environment to expand our usual excessively differentiated ruminating and narrating self, into a transpersonal sense of self that includes our embodied experience, as well as the energy flows and information that we share with others.

3. Consciousness Integration

Interpersonal neurobiology is an interdisciplinary framework that looks for meaningful connections between different fields. By observing that we are complex systems, systems with many interacting parts that are open to chaos and also self-regulating, we can apply related principles to ourselves. Knowing that complex systems function well when their elements are integrated, differentiated and linked, we can do so with intention. By regularly noticing each of your senses individually, including your inner subjective senses, you develop an increasingly refined map of your inner world. This makes responding more appropriately to the outer world much easier. The results of this practice might look like being able to tell the difference between physical hunger and emotional anger: when you are feeling hangry, to then respond appropriately to a friend's text message.

A good place to develop integration is by focusing on the elements that make up your consciousness. Consciousness here is everything you are aware of and your sense of being aware. The content of your awareness is supplied by the senses: hearing (audition), sight (vision), taste (gustation), smell (olfaction), touch (pressure, temperature, light touch, vibration, pain), balance (equilibrioception), position in space (proprioception), sensations inside the body (interoception), as well as your mental/emotional activity and your sense of being in a relationship with others and your environment. Alongside, or perhaps underneath, or just before, this dynamic field of sensory perception is the ever-present, luminous sensation of being aware that you are aware.

4. Heart Coherence and Kind Intention

With all of the senses flooded at a party you have a perfect opportunity to allow awareness to flow between each sense, noticing its distinct qualities and connection to the whole. You can clarify the space between your sensory experience and that underlying luminous sense of being aware that you are aware, the sensation of knowing, of presence. You can solidify this sense of presence through training the mind. The three pillars of mind training are: focused attention, open awareness, and kind intention.[7] On the dancefloor, you train your mind through focused attention on the beat, open awareness to the sensations and experiences that arise, and by holding a kind intention towards yourself and others.

We are usually running on autopilot with our senses and mental activity in their habitual groove, until an experience of awe wakes us up to the lush world beyond our expectations and reconstructions from the past. At first, there is an effort involved in continuously reminding the mind to organize itself around the unfolding present rather than ruminating on the separateness of the self with the Default Mode Network. This ancient network evolved in the nervous system to clarify self and other to increase survival, but it can get out of hand. This story of the self we construct is mutually inhibitory with being a conduit of our sense, and with practice we can influence the flow of our experience. The party makes this process fun, communal, and provides energetic support for the heavy lifting of that internal signal rerouting. Dance loosens the grip of rumination on the self.

Cultivating integration while on the dancefloor is one way to enhance your experience. Coherence is another pathway. Positive emotions increase coherence in heart rate variation, providing an opportunity for global cross-coherence in the body between different systems.[8] The heartbeat is the strongest and most regular electromagnetic signal in the body. When we have consistently positive emotions, the heart rate variation becomes more coherent, that regular signal that reaches the whole body becomes a reference for various body systems to work more harmoniously.

5. An electronic posthuman womb

The space to birth new versions of ourselves is the dancefloor. The rave is an electronic posthuman womb. First, ancestral drums beat polyrhythmically, then the mixer becomes an instrument, sampling stitches together recording sessions on a new timeline, drum machines provide a pulsing permanent present, while turntables infinitely loop the past into the future. The DJ becomes a posthuman channel, their sonic and affective research amplified and mediated through this electronic network. "Womb" because the shared space becomes amniotic. And because the placenta politics of the space embrace difference as a feature, not a glitch, of new life.[9]

And what would have gotten in the way of our amniotic relationship to our environment? Trauma: quotidian trauma, PTSD from acute trauma, social trauma, collective trauma, ancestral trauma. Trauma happens when we have an experience that is too big to hold. We store it in our bodies, knowing it is important, and that we must make sense of it—eventually. But perhaps it is a design flaw, or a design dynamic, that those unintegrated implicit memories can stay that way for the rest of our lives. The dancefloor is a container that is bigger than our trauma.

Traumatic experiences remain undigested until we have the resources to write them into a coherent narrative and feel the big feelings. A party, not as a collection of strangers, but one that has grown through community, becomes a shared resource for us to be held in a space big enough for us to feel bigger than our pain. It is especially good at giving voice to sensations that are difficult to put into words and beyond the reach of language. Well, it can, if we, the party people, use the opportunity of coming together to become more than the sum of our parts. That we may turn up to the party to shift from autopilot to an automatic cascade of non-conceptual presence.[10] Nonconceptual presence is that moment when you awaken from sleeping and for a moment your mind is completely empty, or when the awe of a sunrise stuns you into inner stillness. This is not a fixed state, it is a loosening of our grip on the senses and opening to an underlying ground of being.

We are in an age of paradigm shift from reductionism to one of emergence.[11] We have known this on the dancefloor as a movement toward extended senses, refined senses that are expansive, differentiated from one another and then linked into a more coherent flow than when we got to the party. We can leverage shared intentionality to create enriched environments, integrate our consciousness, and increase heart coherence through kind intention. Regularly reinforcing these pathways and dimensions of experience solidify the state of consciousness into a trait of personality over time.

A state of consciousness includes all of our associations, beliefs, concepts, and emotions in a particular moment. A self-state is a collection of those elements that we return to repeatedly and solidify; the self that shows up on the dancefloor, the self that shows up as a sibling, or as an employee. By acknowledging the seeming paradox of our simultaneous multiplicity of sensory experiences, and the singularity of how they form a coherent whole, we can perceive that our sense of self is also multidimensional. This perspective can then be extended to widen the lens on how we see each other, honoring each other's differences, and allowing the constraints of social lenses to be softened and creatively expanded, giving each other more space for being fully in the complexity of who we are.

6. Mind Training on the Dancefloor
That first moment the party surrounds you, slow down the rhythm of the breath, take in the architecture of the space, let your awareness flow between each of your senses. Feel the sensations on the surface of your skin and ride the flow of sensations arising inside your body. Again, feel the slow, deep rhythm of your breath. Your breath is always with you in this journey.

Here you are, on the dancefloor, letting the beat find its way into your body, taking a few deeper breaths. Feel your sense of inner connection to your body and breath. Feel your sense of interconnection with the other people on the dancefloor. And feel how you are within the vast group of people and lineage of parties that make this moment possible. Be this gratitude, nested in layers of connection.

Once you've been on the dancefloor and you are finding a flow, again focus softly on the sensation of your breath. Then, let your awareness loop from one sense to another. Cycle through the five senses, your position in space, balance, sensations inside the body, mental and emotional activity, and your relational sense of connection with the other people there. This may take a few seconds or a minute or more, but the practice is to take a tour of the senses, notice their continuous unfolding, and eventually, their spaciousness.

On the dancefloor, when you are in your flow, take a few deeper breaths, feel the kind intention in your heart that you and everyone at the party will get free tonight. Let the breath be easy even as it is slow, and your body may be moving quickly, and hold that focus lightly in your awareness.

Deep into the party, again notice the rhythm and sensation of your breath, the flow of your senses, and softly focus your awareness on the space just before the senses arise, the very edge of that wave. Take refuge here. Breathe deeply as you dance on the wave of the senses arising. Be this space.

Moments in Funk

Gavilán Rayna Russom

I used to see a lot of ghosts in the basement space at Tresor.

That's the first sentence of this book I'm slowly writing.

It goes on to talk about how my girlfriend worked the door there and some details about the ghosts

(like how they would appear to be having seizures in the strobe lights).

But I remember this dumb thing from probably middle school about how you should always start a text with a jazzy little titbit that gets peoples' attention and makes them want to read more.

So that's mine.

It merits saying that all of my attempts to find meaning and connection in club and dance music spaces have been hopelessly desperate.

That goes for the uncountable hours I spent following trans women around Berghain and Panorama Bar flirting with them and telling them they were pretty.

Or that summer I lived in Barcelona and that night when I realized the laser in the club was the same color as the absinthe I drank earlier. On the way to the store to buy the absinthe, a sex worker who I had peripherally gotten to know because we frequented the same general spots referred to me as "barba larga con cuerpo de frau"—long beard with a woman's body—or a "frau" body I guess.

Why was her use of German even more affirming than if she'd said "mujer"?

Heading to a gay club tripping on absinthe after that experience, and then the thing with the laser meant that I felt at home both in my body and in the space among others. I enjoyed celebrating and even augmenting that through movements.

And that's one of the things, or maybe the main thing my book would be about:

How I found a home in my body on dancefloors and in club and rave spaces.

A lot of people talk about the value of these spaces as transcendent, and like how they might even say they had "an out of body experience" or an experience that transcended the body or like how they felt like they became one with the music and the people around them . . . and that's not really how it is or was for me.

The repetitive sounds and rhythmic codes, the lights, the people . . . that shit put me *in* my body in a way that felt impossible in other spaces.

Increasingly I understand my experience of being in a body as *inherently* liminal, resonating with what Todd Ramon Ochoa reports that one of his guides in the protocols of Cuban Palo explained to him as "the body being a form of the dead, material insofar as matter was understood as a momentary condensation, precipitation, or coagulation of the fluid immanence of the dead."[1]

Transcription of a voice note entitled "Rhythm is a Dancer" from February 24, 2020:

Ok I don't know why but um. . . book stuff is rolling today in my brain. So, here's a proposal. *Rhythm is a Dancer: The Role of the Body-In-Motion in the Evolution and Innovation of Technomusical Culture.* So, I feel like if I shift my focus and narrow it to talk about this thing of how the dancer, is a composer . . . um . . . of the electronic musical landscape . . . I can talk about a lot of other stuff. And people will know what the fuck I'm talking about.

So, one of the most corrosive aspects of the whitening of the club experience is . . . the . . . What's a good word for that, "pedestalization"? Is the emphasis on the DJ and the DJ's selections as the "artist" and "art object" respectively of the space of cultural consumption that becomes the whitened club. Sooo . . . like I'm proposing to look at it in a more holistic way that, um . . . this is social space there are multiple things happening in it um, and . . . meaning is made, you know. . . as opposed to commodity exchange when um, the club functions as a social whole . . . which comes from Black social life and Black intellectual life, particularly in Detroit in the 1960s, '70s and '80s. Soooo . . . I don't know man, I'm just gonna keep working on this but I feel like that's the focus. That's the focus.

Here are two poems from my book in progress that talk about being in an inherently liminal body on a dancefloor:

1.

My head drops into the depths of my belly. Bells ring. Vines stretch out, thorny, from this new center. Buds grow along the vines. I am star seed. In the ring around my breath is a glowing. She gives herself to the world. She gives herself up to the world. She gives herself down to the underworld. I have roots that touch blood. I have arcs that cross marks on the clock face. Light shuttles along those arcs in sparks. I drink blood through my roots. My head is in my belly. I grew from a tiny pearl near dead. I give blood through my roots. Blood talks. Blood arcs. Sparks arc along blood vines. Everything they're telling me feels wrong in the roots, in the blood, in the blood of the roots. Movement. Arcs of light. She learns her body is a divining rod and an amplifier. Nothing more nothing less. Yes there is a pulse. Tertiary. Blood is first, then sweat. The sweat of others drip blends with hers, with mine. Pulses drip blend. Hearing is tertiary. Body listening is in the center. Body listening through blood.

2.

Heartbeating nearly out of my soaked chest in the hot breath and lights and darkness. Lights in conversation with each other. In the daytime world light is sun or indoor lights designed to allow work to be visible, light is purposed against darkness. Here at night and in this reverberant chamber light and darkness speak to each other; darkness creating permission as it blurs edges and gives cover and light crossing through and articulating shapes in the darkness. In the daytime world light and darkness are a binary and mutually exclude each other. In this world I am being introduced to they are not, they are two elements in conversation from which is born a

third. I sweat and move with others experiencing touch and close-
ness not regimented by binaries of gender and relation. I find there
is respect and appreciation and admiration and joy in the pushing
in the heaving in the sweat. I find there is something in me that
awakens as the temperature of my body increases and that this
awakening is gestural and joyful. I find I am more myself as I am
more in this sound and in this gesture and in this sweat and in this
crowd. I find I am more a woman in this sound, and other women
smile at me. I find I am at home in the darkness through which
lights articulate shape creating a third which is darkness in conver-
sation with light. I find I want this, always.

At some point in late 2009 after moving back to New York from
Berlin I entered a basement space on Broadway in Bushwick.
Growing up in Providence, living in New York in the late '90s and
navigating Berlin's party culture during the five years I lived there, I
spent a lot of time in basement spaces. Basements were frequent
sites for connection, community and enjoyment around music,
especially punk, hardcore, experimental electronics, noise, house
and techno. The basement I entered in 2009, like many I had been
in before, was dark and filled with people whose bodies moved in
time with the repetitive sounds that filled the space. Smoke hung
thick in the air. Individuals in the space entered non-ordinary states
of consciousness, and as I spent more time there, I also began
to enter one. I was not, however, there for a techno party or a
punk show. The smoke that filled the air was from cigars, not a fog
machine. The vocal and rhythmic sounds were made by drummers
and singers rather than a DJ. The ecstatic and trance states that
overtook participants were not the result of drugs but were brought
on through possession by ancestral spirits. This was a Cajon de
Muerto, a Palo drumming ceremony for the dead.

Several things connected for me at this event because of its external similarities to underground electronic music parties. One was that I had been in certain ways searching for something at those parties that they were not capable of providing, whereas the traditional knowledge that held and guided the Cajon de Muerto could. Another was that the dead that filled the room, possessing the bodies of the living and speaking through them were also very present in the sounds, movements, spaces and cultures of electronic dance music in ways that were not often acknowledged.

When I interviewed Cornelius Harris about Underground Resistance, Detroit and Electrifying Mojo, he told me how in the circles he was hanging out in, where the architecture of what would become called techno was being built, folks generally thought of Mojo's approach to selecting tracks as based around one single criterion: "Is it funky?"

Robert Farris Thompson (ibae) glosses the term "funky" in *Flash of the Spirit* as originating in Kongo cosmologies of praise, respect and value, illustrating it in his inimitable way "yati, nkwa lu-fuki! Ve miela miami ikwenda baki (like, there is a really funky person!—my soul advances towards him to receive his blessing)."[2]

"Funky" really is cosmological. What people hear and describe in shorthand as "funky" is multiple instrumental and/or vocal rhythms all "working it out" together in a musical framework which allows these rhythms to conversationally interact with, "bounce off" and inspire each other, simultaneously remaining steady in certain components of their individual identities and changing as a result of those interactions. When the sounds are "funky" there is an opportunity for the social space to be "funky" too. . . for people to interact with each other in complex ways the way the sounds are interacting. Perhaps a truly skilled DJ is less of an "artist" creating an "art object" and more of a creative and spiritual technician, stewarding this kind of "funky" social space.

"Funky" is sounds getting to be together without melting into a singularized whole. Kongo cosmological technology is extremely sophisticated at this kind of holding difference, at creating frameworks where multiple voices can speak with each other, each of them being heard and valued while also retaining their differences. Kongo music models this through polyrhythm and polyvocality, and "funky" is a shorthand for how this feels when you hear it happening.

So here is a small offering, an investigative tool that's been helpful for me and maybe is useful for you as well as you move through the raving landscape. When you are in that raving place . . . the experience you're having . . . is it one of multiple people and energies melting into a single throbbing mass, all focused on the DJ and the music as "artist" and "art object"? Or . . . is it funky?

A San Francisco Ravedream

Chris Zaldua

1.

Am I too old for this shit?

Music is my first love, the single ordering principle of my whole life. All I can really remember about falling in love are the firsts. Like the first time, when I was eight, that I found a cassette tape, which my sister, nearly a decade older, had brought home early in the '90s. Titled *Rave 'til Dawn,* it featured a selection of first-wave Belgian hardcore and breakbeat tracks, whose raw, frenetic sounds pressed a searing brand into my juvenile brain. Growing up in the suburbs, this tape was a portal into another world—one I had no idea existed, but that I desperately needed to know more about.

I listened in secret, after borrowing it—or stealing it—and sequestering myself away in my bedroom. I felt a vivid, all-encompassing sense that by listening, I was engaged in some sort of illicit act, that there was something forbidden and uncouth in this music. It was too brazen—something inherent in its very sound seemed against the law. I felt as if I had been struck by a lightning bolt, and though I couldn't have known it at the time, I would be chasing that dragon ever after.

Then there was the first time I went to a club. I had just returned to the Bay Area after school in Ontario, Canada, my first time living outside of the Bay. Though I had spent years immersing myself in dance music—learning whatever history I could find on the internet, picking and bootlegging favorite tracks—I had never been to a rave. I didn't understand what it meant to "go dancing," which, in my mind, was something that only people who went to their high school prom did. I was well-versed in the multitudes of electronic music in my head, but I was lacking the most fundamental education in the body.

At the time, I had just gotten out of a breakup, and my friend Jon suggested we attend a night called *Warm Leatherette*—named after the iconic post-punk song—at a spot I'd never heard of called Koko's near Geary and Franklin. It's gone now, but back then it was a nondescript dive with taps and bottles and disinterested bartenders serving a motley crowd of local barflies, men wearing 49ers jerseys, and groups of friends celebrating one thing or another.

Off in the corner, I spotted my people immediately: a group of ten or fifteen, crowded around a couple of turntables, blasting wiry synth-punk records to the total disinterest of the rest of the bar. Clad in black, they were arrayed head-to-toe with the subcultural signifiers that I spent my teenage years chasing after, in search of a personality. I lingered nearby with Jon, awkwardly—both of us were terminal internet addicts and had spent the majority of our lives socializing online, to the severe detriment of our interpersonal skills. But a few drinks loosened us up, and we joined the group and met new people.

Even though I hadn't heard any of the records the DJs were playing, they felt intimately familiar, like I had already encountered them in a dream. Each track was riddled with the manic, nervous energy of punk, but carried by an infectious electronic groove, like the electronic body music and proto-techno I had known and loved growing up. I had stumbled upon some kind of missing link.

Toward the end of the night, one of the DJs played the Dutch electro anthem "Space Invaders Are Smoking Grass," a track I had only ever heard at home, by myself—but never on a night out and certainly never in this context, sandwiched between raucous, wavy songs by disaffected European youth. Suddenly, I got it. The track sounded different, felt different. I was gripped by an unfamiliar energy. Listening amongst this tiny crowd of weirdos I had just met, I got what I had been missing out on, what I had lost by sitting at home with headphones: that music is so much more than an art form—it's a social binder, an aural glue that brings people together and ties them up in community.

I went up to the DJ and thanked him, told him I loved this track, that I had never heard it mixed with others like these before. He told me his name: Nihar. He was tall and deftly bearded with an unhinged frizz of curly hair, like Jack Nance from *Eraserhead* if Jack were brown, and he wore a torn and faded t-shirt bearing the insignia of some punk or metal band I had never heard of. That he was a DJ, even if just a hobbyist, seemed thrillingly cool to me, and shockingly accessible. In my naive mind, DJs were mythical figures, the stuff of legend: DJing was the province of Jeff Mills or Richie Hawtin, people whose mix CDs I'd find for sale in the racks at Amoeba. But I had it all wrong, of course—it was the amateurs who had always run the show. I didn't know it then, but Nihar would become one of my best friends and longest-running musical collaborators. More and more would appear the deeper I immersed myself in the local scene.

Soon came my first underground parties—literally underground: beneath a curio shop on 24th; in the basement of an illegal club on 6th; down some horrifically unsafe stairs at 17th and Capp. At these spots I danced myself into a stupor for the first time. I stayed 'til the lights came on, and then time and time again. At these spots I shared a kiss on the dancefloor for the first time: one night after *Icee Hot* in the Loft at Public Works was done, Jenna dragged me to a warehouse several blocks north on Mission Street, where she and I embraced one another amongst hundreds of sweaty harness-bound men, all of us pulsing as one solid mass past 4 a.m. And at these spots I did drugs for the first time: I swallowed a clear gel caplet—"moon rocks," or so my friend said—and I ended the night being driven around in the back of a van containing dozens of CRT TVs that had lit up the party just hours before, laughing myself into oblivion.

Eventually, I played my first DJ set. Because I spent so long without ever really going out, my relationship with DJing was abstracted, too—it had never occurred to me that I might try it myself. But my friends kept telling me: "You like a bunch of good music, and you should play it out some time," and I realized it really is that simple.

That night I took the stage and played a series of records to a very small crowd for the very first time. I insisted on mixing vinyl, the mark of an insecure amateur, and I trainwrecked half the mixes, lacking in both confidence and technical skill. But on a few cuts, I nailed the timing just right, seamlessly blending one track with another, and it felt like alchemy. Looking out amongst the meager crowd, I saw wonder on their faces, the joy of musical discovery happening in real time. I was hooked.

Not long after, I took the next logical step: I started a new party, for the first time, with my newfound friends. I'd been going to *Warm Leatherette* for years and had befriended all the DJs. For months, I'd send them techno tracks I thought would fit amongst their usual post-punk and minimal synth selections. The one that really landed was a squirrelly acid roller by Cassegrain and Tin Man called "Athletic"—when they played it out, it was clear the vibe had shifted. Soon enough, I was sitting for brunch at an Irish pub on 22nd and Guerrero with Nihar, Jason, Justin, Andreas, and Damon, chatting through the vision of a techno party that possessed the raw, punk-ish energy that *Warm Leatherette* did, and I suggested a name: *Surface Tension*. It stuck, and we were all in.

2.

In a DJ set, you rarely hear the beginning of a track—usually just the middle, when it's already come into its own. In the beginning, nobody in San Francisco knew who I was, but in the span of a few years, I had gone from diehard raver to amateur DJ to party promoter. I wrote a weekly dance music column in *SF Weekly*, and had bylines in *XLR8R*, *Resident Advisor,* and Red Bull Music Academy. My social circle expanded ever wider until I, a lifelong shut-in, had more acquaintances than I knew what to do with. For the first time in my life, I had become somebody.

Thinking back, those days hardly seem real. Hollowed out after the comorbid crashes of 2008, the city was bursting at the seams with stylish, creative people everywhere I looked. Rent wasn't exactly cheap, but we made it work. Everyone I met was a musician, an artist, a photographer, or a designer; everyone worked at a bar, a restaurant, a gallery, or a clothing store. There were parties every weekend: in houses, in backyards, in lofts, in clubs that had just opened. Neighborhoods were rife with happening and buzzing with collaborative, productive energy.

For a while, at least, *Surface Tension* stood alone in San Francisco. We curated the party without compromise, seeking a common thread between the chaotic weirdness of experimental music and the kinetic dynamism of dance music. We mixed crowds, scenes, and sounds, building lineups you'd find nowhere else in the city. It didn't always work out—sometimes, both audiences and venues alike were bewildered by what we put on stage—but when the energy was on, we pierced the veil between noise and techno, art and club.

In the meantime, I earned a steady stream of gigs, but I was paid just barely enough to keep my head above water. I was fueled by the sense that my lucky break would come—if the right people read my writing, maybe, or if I just made the right connections. In my spare time, I dreamt about trading the exhausting freelance grind for a stable creative career. What that looked like I couldn't have told you, but I believed that if I worked hard enough and put the time in, I would find my big break.

But the grind wore me down, and the crushing weight of my own jadedness became harder and harder to ignore. It felt like every booking, every event, every endeavor was a numbers game: *OK, but how many will we get through the door? And will they drink enough to clear the bar minimum?* I began to understand the music business as, effectively, a subsidiary of the alcohol business, and I began to ask myself: *What am I doing this for?*

Each passing month, another friend or connection would depart for Berlin, New York, or Los Angeles. In their stead came transplants, new to the city, wearing Allbirds and backpacks emblazoned with their employers' logos, lining up on street corners to board gleaming white double-decker chariots that ferried them down 280 to corporate campuses where they built out our new world with wireframes and code. Along with them came ads in BART stations and on Muni buses featuring phrases like "onboarding," "deployment," and "enterprise-level security."

One day, in the café where I did my writing, I noticed a curious plastic contraption with phone-charging cables emerging from it every which way, like anime tentacles. A startup was selling subscriptions to charge your phone—never mind that this café was flush with outlets visitors could use for free. In another café, an old-school place run by a Vietnamese family, I went to use the bathroom only to discover its traditional wooden door had been replaced by a metal one, institutional-looking but painted a jarring lime green, with a bulging hotel-style lock. Some other startup was paying local cafés around the city—who were struggling with skyrocketing costs of doing business—to commandeer their bathrooms, charging patrons a subscription fee to use them.

Rent-seeking had given way to toilet-seeking.

At some point or another, I could no longer ignore the signs that something in the city had changed materially. Whatever windows of opportunity I had hoped to climb through, toward whatever creative career I had dreamed of, were shuttering rapidly—or were simply mirages to begin with.

3.

Then came lockdown. Events disappeared overnight, as did my participation in the music industry. I spent over two years in a miasmic void of numbness and total uncertainty, and at its peak, when it felt like the walls had closed all the way in, I could imagine no way out—that there would never be any "going back to normal." What I couldn't tell you was if 'back to normal" was something I wanted. I had spent so long rolling the boulder uphill, oftentimes for little more than the thrill of a good night—and those memories don't pay the bills. Here was my chance: I could just walk away.

But I didn't. As San Francisco began to emerge from its social coma in the middle of 2022, perhaps the last major city in the U.S. to do so, I began going out once again—if less than I used to—and I began co-producing a monthly party called *Vague Terrain* once again, starting over essentially from scratch.

Going out was bewildering at first: a very particular flavor of déjà vu that didn't exist pre-pandemic, folding in on itself amidst childlike wonder. But I struggled then, and struggle now, with a terrible sinking feeling that comes from bleeding money and toiling for hours producing an event only to walk away with little or nothing in your pocket. It isn't exactly work you can retire on. I found myself asking the same questions as before: Why do I put in the work? Why do I put up with the bullshit? Why do I still show up?

I think back, as I often do, to those friends I lost on December 2, 2016. A fire during a rave in the Oakland warehouse Ghost Ship took the lives of thirty-six people; my friends counted dozens among the dead. I was at a DIY show in Jack London Square that night, about to head to the party, until my friend Sara sent me a burst of texts in a row: "There's a fire at Ghost Ship," she said. "It's bad. Don't go."

Immediately in its wake, I poured everything I had into telling their stories to anyone who would listen. I had never written an obituary before, but within two weeks, I wrote four. I spoke on the radio and agreed to reporters' interview requests. I penned articles for newspapers and magazines in a meager attempt to correct the narrative: that the event that night wasn't a commercially-driven "EDM concert," nor was it a drug-addled bacchanal, but a gathering of like-minded outsiders sharing their artistry with one another for its own sake.

A year after the fire, I wrote a letter to my friend Johnny, a DJ and musician who we lost that night. "I've been thinking a lot about grief. Does it ever go away?" I wrote then. I know now that it does not—it just changes shape. Through a nonlinear process, acts of commemoration and mutual aid bridge the chasm of loss, osmosing anguish and despair into kinship and, eventually, into celebration.

Last year, we hosted *Vague Terrain* on the seventh anniversary of the fire, the first time that our standing monthly date ever landed on December 2. At first, we were uncertain how to proceed: Should we cancel the party? Host a memorial? We decided to move forward—what those no longer with us would have wanted—and booked Nihar, friend and comrade, for a live performance, and Kiernan Laveaux, a thrillingly talented selector from Cleveland, to close out the night. The mood was ecstatic, and when the lights came on, I remembered: That in spite of all the bullshit, to gather together—to find community in one another, between each other—matters so much more than we know.

I am attuned, now, to a kind of gratitude. When a friend tells me they had forgotten how vital it is to see so many other friends all at once, I bask in it; when another friend tells me that our party feels like an expression of our personalities, that who we are shines through in our booking and production, I revel in it. And at the end of the night, when a friend, drenched in sweat from dancing, tells me how much they needed that, I am aglow.

This gratitude has always been there, of course. It's the fundament of the rave. It's something primal. Maybe today, though, it is more freely given, since it seemed, for a moment, that it could all disappear.

And so to answer to answer my own rhetorical question, I am not yet too old for this shit, no. Someday maybe, but not today. I'll see you on the dancefloor.

Safe Home

Shawn Dickerson

I never went to Studio 54. For me that was aspirational. Looking at it in magazines, I'd imagine I'd go to New York and go there. But I was too young. I missed it by a few yeawrs. It was '78-'79 and I was still in high school, but I was fantasizing about it a lot.

I got to New York when I was about 21. I was in Florida for college, and I just felt—ugh— about it. I would come up here to see this kid from Florida who lived on the Upper West Side and worked at this club called Xenon. I would hang out with him while he'd be working, and I would talk to people to try to find where the gay people hung out. I went to Uncle Charlie's. I started seeing the whole gay scene. I decided to leave Florida and come to New York.

That's when I started going to Paradise Garage and Area. The thing about Garage, that whole experience, is that everybody was just hanging out together. It wasn't about you being different to the other person. Like, how I met Keith Haring: He was just smoking this joint outside, and this guy walked by, really cute, and we both came in looking for him, and Keith smiled at me. We laughed and he asked if I wanted some of his joint. And then we would just kick it like that.

I guess I knew he was an artist, but he never really talked about that with me. I would see him hang out with certain people, but really everyone hung out with everyone, so you didn't really know who anybody really was. Unless they were *really* famous. He was on the cusp then. I remember going to this art opening. I walk in and he's there. He catches me staring at him. He turned to me and we start laughing. Like the same way he always was. He was like, "oh, you didn't know?" And I'm like, "No, queen."

Keith was definitely part of the Garage scene. I had this moment of thinking that I wasn't in the inner circle for a while, and I wondered if he was one of the people I wanted to get to know. I'd seen Grace Jones walk through, and I'm thinking: "what's going on here?" Then there'd be Madonna, with all the bracelets on, like 'Lucky Star,' all that, and I'd be—"what's going on?" She'd just taken off. That's how it was. Whoever was going to do whatever they did, they did it. But Keith was someone you could just get to know and it'd be cool. He was one of the people I just wanted to hang out with. I remember taking a seat at Danceteria, and he'd come over to see me and my friends, warmly and honestly.

When I think back about the Garage moment, I guess that's why people are interested in my story. I was around Basquiat and all those people. But I was so fucking young and just caught up in living that New York moment. Being twenty-two in New York and finding yourself. Playing with all this new stuff. Like we had these friends who were African Royalty, they had diplomatic immunity, but they were drug addicts. All of a sudden limousines are coming to pick them up. Hanging out with Marci Klein and she's telling you stories about her father—Calvin. It was stuff like that all the time. I was so busy getting high. I was *living*.

I want people to know about those times and think about it. But honestly, I think the kids now, in this moment, are creating a moment like the one I saw. I feel it. I've lived through it enough. I've felt it happen a few times. And they're just doing their shit and living their lives. *That* one is going out and getting fucked up or whatever, but they're going to be the next William Burroughs.

I was at Fashion Institute of Technology back then. I'd hang out getting dressed for hours. You'd have three or four looks before you. I'd be with my best friend of the time. Louis was the reason I'd come to New York. He decided he wanted to create this drag personality called Mercy Jones. He would be dressing up for *hours*. Teasing his hair. He was Italian, really beautiful. We'd been dressing with each other for years. We go out about five-thirty or six and stay 'til the end, which was usually about twelve. We'd hang out with the Xtravaganzas who'd all leave the club and go hang out by the Piers. That'd be your Saturday and Sunday. The Xtravaganzas used to scare me a little bit.

When I was growing up in Philly my grandmother had this best friend George who was a transvestite and who hung out with this really flamboyant friend, Tommy. The whole setting was that my grandmother ran a speakeasy. They'd all hang out at my grandmother's speakeasy. Tommy would come over and get dressed up and be there in her clothes, would tell stories and entertain. Tommy had lived in New York. Everyone just drinking and laughing. My grandmother loved it.

I was a kid, and George and Tommy would tease me until I'd be crying. I was always scared of anything too fast. Or too flamboyant. I think I'm different now but then it freaked me out. It was scary. They would tease the fuck out of me. I'd have a friend with me who was just a friend and they'd be like "Is that your *boyfriend*?" I'd be like, "I'm not gay!" and they'd be like, "queen…" I'd call my grandmother over to protect me. I kind of grew up with that.

In school, all my friends came out when we were in the ninth grade. I always thought that if someone is comfortable enough telling me their secret then who am I to judge? Who am I to refuse accept- ance? It was always that way. Whatever it was, I'd be like, OK, that's cool. My best friend Louis would take me to the park they called Judy Garland Park, that's where they'd cruise. He'd take me there. He'd say, "sit over there on the bench and watch out for the police." I was always the lookout. It wasn't until years later that I realized that I was putting myself in these situations because I was curious. At the time it didn't feel like my thing.

Maybe it's a socio-economic thing. Like, my friend Lisa. She was really young when she started dressing up. She had a twin sister and started dressing like her sister. We lived in a tough neighbor- hood, but she'd be there in her outfits. Just to say that I was being butch, but they were the ones fighting battles. I was not. All these things are lessons I learned that have really served me in what I do now. I feel like it's given me access to this next generation that a lot of people that are my age don't have. I've always accepted people as they are.

When I got to New York from Florida, the look was *preppy*. It was boat shoes. I was so into Polo, in matching colors. But then in my head I was a fucking freak. I was encouraging Louis to do looks but I was never comfortable, although as I got older I got more and more comfortable. When I was at FIT, when we'd go out to the Garage, I'd first start dressing preppy like that, but Louis would be like, "wear a skirt!" I worked in the knitwear lab, and I'd make these long skirts. I always liked what I called the "Olive Oyl look." Really long, long skirt, a big puffer jacket. And then I started wearing wigs, with hats on top of the wigs. I would just play around with it a lot.

It was interesting because when I was dressed like this, boys hit on me. Different types of people would try to talk to me. I would get different types of attention. I think all of that was also me experimenting with that thing about how people judge you, how people would judge me. But the reality is, that's your bullshit, that's your movie. I'm the same person right here. It's all your projections.

Now I dress more like I used to when I dressed down. If I'm working three nights in a row, there's usually one night I'll not wear glasses, one where I wear glasses, or sometimes I wear fake glasses. If I wear the black one night I'll wear color the next. I do love wearing skirts and I do love that at the door. When I put it on, it doesn't feel like I'm trying to be feminine, it just feels like it takes away the power of this item. There's this whole door thing were as door you're judging someone and at the same time they're judging me. I always think that's interesting, they're like looking at me like, "what are you wearing, girl?"

I started working door in the '80s. I'd met my first boyfriend, Joe, and we lived in the East Village. Thursday nights we would always go to Boy Bar, which was on St. Marks. After a few months they asked me to work there. That's where I started. That was probably 1984. I was really young, early twenties. Then after Boy Bar we'd walk down the Bowery, going to the Garage. It was seedy down there then. I'd be getting into situations with homeless people along the way and Joe would be like, "let's just get to the club!"

We'd get there, and Patricia Field would be sitting there. There was this connection between Patricia and Larry Levan, through this guy who worked for her, who like Larry was into dope. Larry was the star of the Garage. I started hanging out with him. There was this whole fashion connection. What's interesting is that I think the same fashion-club connection is happening now. I see these young kids—I'm fascinated by them. They look like they're deconstructed, or just falling apart, but then you look closer at the outfit and its labels and like, "girl, *what* are you doing? Girl rent is expensive. I don't know what you're doing to afford to look like that!" That's what I love about the city. There's so many stories.

I've worked door pretty much non-stop since Boy Bar days. I was doing that when Joe said: "why not start a club?" He started Café Con Leche, and I worked it with him. And that segued into Starlight Wonderbar. I put in about ten years there. Then The Cock. Everybody would hang out there. Then bigger clubs, like Twilo.

The thing about the bigger clubs: Joe would say, "you're too small for the bigger clubs." They wanted that thing that I don't really do. The big tough thing, whereas for me door is more psychological. I guess it's like from the time I was with my grandmother, because back then I would see the whole night. I'd see how, like this one is getting riled up. As I got a bit older my grandmother and I would have signals, like, "watch that one!" I just got good at seeing people. Most people, when there is a situation, they just want to be heard. I've seen it so many times. The way they're making it physical, it so didn't need to be physical. So the bouncing thing is not really for me.

In terms of today's parties, when I work those T4T parties, it feels like there's a real reason for me to be there. I can make someone feel comfortable in a way other people can't. That's my gift, my "superpower." It feels very natural to me. And I think it's important. In terms of clubs that are hard to get into, I was never really involved with those types of door. All that shady door stuff, like at Twilo or Sound Factory, was all performative. At the end of the day, that performance about keeping people out made people want to come to that club. It's the same shit now.

The underground techno parties that I work we do try to keep out a certain kind of vibe. If people don't get in, it's usually based on entitlement. If you're too much with us, then we're going to get into it. Sometimes I work with Cedric, and I feel that his door is different. He's very good at treating people well, but when he gets shady, it's like a performance. We've talked about it. He'll say, "I have an avatar. This is my avatar for the night." Us working together, I learned some of that style.

Working Basement door has changed me a lot. There's a speed of decision there. The security guys always laugh at it. Like I'll say to someone "Oh I love your jacket," but the next things is "thank you so much for coming, but another time." The security guys are like, "you just smiled at that person's jacket and turned them away, how do you do that?" Because it's not personal. I really liked that jacket. It's just really fast there. Those Basement nights, that's thousands of people. I don't know how many people I've interacted with at the door, a few hundred thousand, easy.

I think in terms of how to manage people's expectations. That came from watching my grandmother. I would watch her deal with problems. Throwing people out. There was so much shade going on. She would have this whole signal system. And they'd put wider straws in some drinks, so people would drink them faster. If someone got too drunk and they were by themselves, you know someone would lift his wallet. It'd be crazy. He'd be getting into it with my grandmother, and she'd be saying, "you accuse *me* of stealing?" When the whole time she had it.

It's funny like every time I go to Berlin, I look at how the door feels. We always get this whole comparison with Berlin, as if Basement was Berghain. But it's never going to be. The way Americans react to that "no" at the door, that's such a different thing. In Germany people just walk away. They've been doing it such a long time. Here it's like, "you're going to do this to *me*?"

I'll say this: there's certain nights particularly when I've had a really long shift, and I have to work the next night. When I'm just *over it*. Someone comes up, and I'll try to be sweet, but I just want it over. I'm like, "what do you need?" Let's get this over. Let's get you in or get you out. How you do this depends on where you're at. Do you have support there? That varies. Sometimes it's like: "let's just talk over here." A lot of it is listening. The thing that's really important is that anyone who's inside, or who's in the perimeter of what's going on, like smoking a cigarette or whatever, I want the situation to be as minimal as possible for them. The people around shouldn't even know it's happening.

It's funny, like the other day, Cedric and I had a situation. You could see it was happening. Later I was told it was GHB. I didn't even know this person did G. Maybe he'd just been drinking. He was slurring and talking to himself. I saw that and I thought: he looks like something is happening to him. You keep an eye on someone like that. He went back in, came back out. I was dealing with something else. Cedric was talking to him. I said to Cedric, "I think you should walk him down a little bit." He'd be saying, "I'm gonna leave, I'm gonna leave," and then he'd sit down and start to pray. He was in this loop, of getting up and talking, getting on his knees, praying. Sometimes we have to deal with things like that. You're trying to get them to go home. You're just trying to get them to a safe place. It was a good hour with him. We're trying to get him hydrated this whole time with citrus and water. Finally he was able to get it together enough to go home. That's the part I don't want you to see.

It's crazy on a [Redacted] night at [Redacted]. I would hate to be an EMT at that party. It's the worst job ever. But a lot of places don't want to be like the TSA at the airport. You know why people are there. But with the G thing, it really is problematic because I just don't see people controlling it. They're always doing too much or not dosing properly or mixing it with other things. It's hard when you're in that state to say no.

I did this one party, it's a younger crowd. Those kids are really young. It's quiet the first hour as there's nobody there. This doll shows up, she's zooted up, she's tells me this and that and her whole thing. But you know, I had to ride the ride and be on that show with her. Sometimes you're not there, but they are, so they have you.

Sometimes when I don't have to be on the door I like just walking through and dancing. Sometimes I'm checking to see how the vibe is. That's part of the whole thing with working door. You have to see what it feels like. Does it need more of this or less of this? Sometimes I wish I could get in to dance sooner. I've had some DVS1 evenings where—ah! I just want to get in there and get to it.

It's a hard door to work, but I love dancing to Carry Nation. That door is challenging because a lot of regular Greenpoint people go to Good Room. Some of them tend to be bros and they just really want to be in there. They're fighting to get in. I can try to convince them not to want it. I don't mind taking the straight dollar for the club, but sometimes they're going to pay thirty dollars, and they're going to stay less than thirty minutes.

Or sometimes the gay kids will be like, "there's too many girls!" But there's too many everything. One of the lines I really hate hearing from straight people on the door is "well how bad is it?" Then I have to tell them "It's not for you." There's nothing bad about this, it's just not for you if you say that to me. Or they'll ask, "Is it *really*, really gay?"

There was one guy, he was the cutest too, almost like a young JFK Jr. He came up with two girls and a guy, like two couples. He asks, "do you think I'd have fun?" I can't tell you that. He's asking, "is it just too many guys?" I'm pointing to the girl he's with and saying, "you probably won't get hit on," and I'm saying to him, "you will *definitely* get hit on." Does that work for you? This is going to be part of the experience." I ended up telling him, "it's a little too gay *even for me*." And he says, "right on!" We laughed about it.

Now that I'm taking acting lessons I'm thinking about what acting is all about. You're creating this exceptional thing that sometimes feels as unreal as possible, and making it a reality. That's sometimes where you're at with the club. There's so many shenanigans. There's so many levels. People are coming up to you. Like sometimes you're in space. Sometimes people are including you in whatever is going on in their head. Particularly at Basement. There's videos and posts from people we rejected. I try to tell everybody at door, just try to come together for a moment, and see where they're at, see if they know the DJs. See if they're part of the community but just look different tonight. Some people are mad because they paid for an Uber to get there. That entitlement thing.

I've been doing this for so long. I'm imagining myself *not* doing it. I'll move myself out of it. After Starlight, I started trying other things, as I'd done that for ten years straight. Someone would ask, "can you do this one party?" I did one party and then they wanted me for [Redacted]. That was my transition from the house and gay world to the techno underground thing. That led to Basement, [Redacted] and now those [redacted] kids want me to do a party with them in Berlin.

I think about how you document all this. My ex, he was obsessed with documenting the Garage. It goes back to my grandmother again. When I was a kid all she talked about was how Billie Holiday was so great in her day and I'd be like "will you shut up about Billie Holiday!" I love Billie Holiday now. For me back then it was like "girl, okay, that was your moment, *live*. This is *my* moment." I'd be trying to tell her about the Garage, and she'd be "well back in my day…."

I think about this a lot. You know the Pepper Labejia scene in *Paris is Burning*? Where she's like, "I've had a good life." I really feel that. The resignation of that. Particularly as you get older. Thinking about my uncle George and his best friend Tommy who used to tease me. They were getting sick. My grandmother was trying to be there for them. They were basically without family. I was so scared of that.

What was always important to me is that I had really good relationships with people. My chosen family became my real family. We were there for each other. But I get really inspired by the kids now. They're just free in a way that's kind of astonishing. Sometimes I'm shocked by it, but I'm just really happy for them. I just want people to be accepted. If I give anything to anybody, it's that. And to get home safe.

Contributors

Afsana Mousavi: But secretly you'd love to know what it's like, wouldn't you? What it feels like for a girl.

Alice Hines is a journalist in New York City.

Artist and poet **Anne Lesley Selcer** is the author of *Sun Cycle*, an investigation into visual beauty, and *Blank Sign Book*, a collection of essays on art & politics.

Brittany Newell is a writer, performer, party thrower and professional dominatrix living in San Francisco. Her new novel *Soft Core* was published in February 2025. by FSG in the US, Harper Collins in the UK, and Fayard in France.

Chris Zaldua is a writer, DJ, nightlife organizer, and record label co-founder based in San Francisco, CA.

cranberry thunderfunk, also known as Tim, is a dancer, writer, and artist living in Ithaca, NY.

Destiny Be is a multi-media artist living in Brooklyn, New York.

E.R. Pulgar is a Venezuelan American poet, journalist, and translator. They have published two chapbooks: *Sonnet to the Serpent and Other Poems* (Wonder) and a translation of Isadoro Saturno's *Dear Parent or Guardian* (UDP).

Ev Delafose is a writer and scholar who focuses on Black queer and trans art, design, fashion, and culture. Their current and upcoming research projects focus on Blackness, transness, aesthetics, and beingness.

Frankie Wiener is a genderqueer artist, teacher and student of Judaic studies, nightlife worker and dance floor freak based in NYC.

Gavilán Rayna Russom is a visionary artist, scholar and curator based in New York City whose work provides alternatives to binary thought and categorization. She is also the founding director of Voluminous Arts.

Geoffrey Mak is the author of *Mean Boys: A Personal History.*

hannah baer is a writer and clinical psychologist based in New York. She is the author of the memoir *trans girl suicide museum.* Her second book, Life of the Party, will be published by MCD in 2027.

Harry Burke is an art critic and a PhD candidate in art history at Yale University, New Haven.

Isabelia Herrera writes about femme aesthetics and Caribbean diasporas in electronic music, dembow, and reggaeton. She is a critic and curator based in Brooklyn.

Journey Streams is a writer, performer, and nightlife historian based in Brooklyn.

Kumi James, aka BAE BAE, is a Los Angeles based DJ, sound artist, organizer, and PhD candidate in Media Arts & Practice. She organizes innovative communal spaces, including the notorious LA black & brown queer underground party, *HOOD RAVE.*

Linn Tonstad is professor of theology, religion, and sexuality at Yale Divinity School and a devoted raver.

madison moore is an assistant professor of Modern Culture and Media at Brown University and is currently writing a book about queer nightlife.

DJ, producer, and antidisciplinary artist **MORENXXX**, aka **Jesús Hilario-Reyes**, situates their practice at the crossroads of sonic performance, land installation, and sculpture, their iterative works examine carnival and rave culture throughout the West.

McKenzie Wark is the author of *Raving, Reverse Cowgirl* and various other things.

MX Oops is an assistant professor of Dance, Multimedia Performance, and Somatic Studies in the Department of Music, Multimedia, Theatre, and Dance at Lehman College, CUNY. Their work centers hybridity, encouraging ecstatic disobedience as a path toward embodied wellness.

Shawn Dickerson: I'VE WORKED NIGHTLIFE THE PAST FORTY YEARS, AND WORKED IN FASHION BEFORE MOVING TO THE ARTWORLD NOW MY DAYJOB IS ACTING WHILE MY NIGHTS ARE FILLED WORKING DOOR AT THE BEST TECHNO PARTIES IN TOWN

Simon Wu is a writer and curator. His first book, *Dancing On My Own*, was published with Harper Collins in 2024.

Slant Rhyme is an artist and writer. Her work spans video, text-based performance, and image production. She lives and works in Brooklyn, NY.

Zora Jade Khiry is a fountain of blood in the shape of a girl. She lives in Brooklyn atop a tree which grows hearts. Black people <3 Waywardness <3 Techno <3.

Zoë Beery is a journalist covering the radical edges of social, economic, and cultural change, and a nightlife harm reduction organizer at parties, clubs and festivals in the U.S. and Europe.

Zoey Greenwald is a writer and editor based between Los Angeles and New York.

Endnotes

Introduction

1   DeForrest Brown Jr, *Assembling a Black Counterculture* (Brooklyn: Primary Information, 2022).

When Din Becomes Discourse

1   Eduard Glissant, *Caribbean Discourse: Selected Essays* (Charlottesville: University Press of Virginia, 1989), 122.

Civilization and its Discothèques

1   Dominic Pettman, *After the Orgy: Towards a Politics of Exhaustion* (Albany: SUNY Press, 2002), 162.

We Can All Live in This House

1   Livy, *The History of Rome*, Book 39.

2   The slogan of Dweller 3: https://dwellerforever.club/dweller-3.

Seedlings

1   Henri Lefebvre, *Rhythmanalysis* (London: Continuum), 2004, 76-77

A Politics for the End of The World

1   I borrow the phrase "the end of the world as we know it" from Denise Ferreira da Silva in her essay "Toward a Black Feminist

Poethics: The Quest(ion) of Blackness Toward the End of the World," 2014. Her writing and thinking about a Black Feminist poethic praxis helped to guide this essay's conjuring.

2   I am using this term as described by Edward Soja in *Thirdspace: Journey to Los Angeles and Other Real-and-Imagined Places*, 1996.

3   Hortense J. Spillers, "Mama's Baby, Papa's Maybe: An American Grammar Book," *Diacritics*, Vol. 7, no. 2, Summer 1987.

4   Ishmael Reed, *Mumbo Jumbo* (New York: Scribner, 1996).

5   "As a culture worker who belongs to an oppressed people my job is to make revolution irresistible." —Toni Cade Bambara

Adult Entertainment

1   Angela McRobbie, *Feminism and Youth Culture* (New York: Red Globe Press, 2000); Dick Hebdige, *Subculture: The Meaning of Style* (Oxford: Routledge, 1979); and Sarah Thornton, *Club Cultures* (Middletown: Wesleyan University Press, 1995).

2   Michel Foucault, "Friendship as a Way of Life," *Ethics: Subjectivity and Truth* (New York: The New Press, 1994), 138.

3   Kemi Adayemi, *Feels Right: Black Queer Women and the Politics of Partying in Chicago* (Durham: Duke University Press, 2022).

4   Johan Huizinga, "Nature and Significance of Play as a Cultural Phenomenon" in *Homo Ludens: A Study of the Play-Element in Culture* (Oxford: Routledge, 1946), 8; 158.

Dancing Lonely: Becoming Black, Queer, and Trans

1   Leo Bersani, "Sociability and Cruising," in *Australian and New Zealand Journal of Art* 3, no. 1 (2002): 11–31.

2   Ibid, 47.

3   Ibid, 47.

4   Marlon M. Bailey, *Butch Queens Up in Pumps: Gender, Performance, and Ballroom Culture in Detroit* (Ann Arbor: University of Michigan Press, 2013), 54.

5   Jafari S. Allen, *There's a Disco Ball Between Us: A Theory of Black Gay Life* (Durham: Duke University Press, 2022), 5.

6   Hester Baer. "Redoing Feminism" in *Feminist Media Studies* 16, no. 1 (2016): 17-34, 21.

Ecstatic Aesthetics: Mind Training on the Dancefloor

1   M. Tomasello, *Becoming Human: A Theory of Ontogeny* (Cambridge: Belknap Press, 2019).

2   D. J. Siegel, *Pocket guide to Interpersonal Neurobiology: An Integrative Handbook of the Mind* (New York: W. W. Norton, 2012), 23-2.

3   A. C. Kentner, et al., "Editorial: Environmental Enrichment: Enhancing Neural Plasticity, Resilience, and Repair," in *Frontiers in Behavioral Neuroscience*, vol. 13, 2019.

4   S. Magsamen and I. Ross, *Your Brain on Art: How the Arts Transform Us* (New York: Random House, 2023).

5   Siegel, *Pocket Guide to Interpersonal Neurobiology*, 1-11.

6   D. J. Siegel, *IntraConnected: MWe (Me + We) as the Integration of Self, Identity, and Belonging* (New York: W. W. Norton, 2022).

7   D. J. Siegel, *Aware: The Science and Practice of Presence* (New York: TarcherPerigee, 2018), 46.

8   R. McCraty, *Science of the Heart, Volume 2: Exploring the Role of the Heart in Human Performance* (Heartmath, 2015), 24.

9   R. Braidotti, *Posthuman Feminism* (Cambridge: Polity Books, 2022), 170.

10   J. H. Austin, *Zen-Brain Horizons: Toward a Living Zen* (Cambridge: MIT Press, 2014), 155.

11   V. McCabe, *Coming to Our Senses: Perceiving Complexity to Avoid Catastrophe* (Oxford: Oxford University Press, 2014).

Moments in Funk

1   Todd Ramon Ochoa, *Society of the Dead: Quita Manaquita and Palo Praise in Cuba* (Oakland: University of California Press, 2010)

2   Robert Farris Thompson, *Flash of the Spirit: African and Afro-American Art and Philosophy* (New York: Vintage, 1984).